RETHINKING THE PATRIOT ACT

We aren't good at sifting thru info we have. Add to that now having to tell if the info is true or false – can't presume veracity the way you can when listening to a convo b/w 2 ppl who don't know they're being surveilled

This effort is part of The Century Foundation's Homeland Security Project, a broader study aimed at informing the public and the policy-making community about the complex challenges related to preventing and responding to domestic terrorism. The Century Foundation gratefully acknowledges the support for its Homeland Security Project by the John D. and Catherine T. MacArthur Foundation, the John S. and James L. Knight Foundation, the Robert Wood Johnson Foundation, and the Carnegie Corporation of New York. More information on the project is available at www.tcf.org and www.homelandsec.org.

STEPHEN J. SCHULHOFER

RETHINKING
THE PATRIOT ACT

Keeping America Safe and Free

A Century Foundation Report

The Century Foundation Press • New York

The Century Foundation sponsors and supervises timely analyses of economic policy, foreign affairs, and domestic political issues. Not-for-profit and nonpartisan, it was founded in 1919 and endowed by Edward A. Filene.

LIBRARY OF CONGRESS CATALOGING-IN-PUBLICATION DATA

Schulhofer, Stephen J.
  Rethinking the Patriot Act : keeping America safe and free / Stephen J. Schulhofer.
      p. cm.
  Includes bibliographical references and index.
  ISBN 0-87078-495-1 (pbk. : alk. paper)
  1. United States. Uniting and Strengthening America by Providing Appropriate Tools Required to Intercept and Obstruct Terrorism (USA PATRIOT ACT) Act of 2001. 2. National security—Law and legislation—United States. 3. Terrorism—United States—Prevention. 4. Civil rights—United States. I. Title.
  KF4850.A3125 S38 2005
  345.73'02—dc22

                                        2005009925

10 9 8 7 6 5 4 3 2 1

FOREWORD

Over the course of the nearly four years since the September 11 terrorist attacks, the U.S. government has responded with periodic bursts of dramatic action, including enactment of the Patriot Act, the invasions of Afghanistan and Iraq, the creation of the federal Department of Homeland Security, and the recent reorganization of the nation's intelligence bureaucracy. It will be some time before we can assess the full impact of these developments, especially their long-term consequences for the security of the United States. And, in the short run, our ability to critique or praise them is limited severely by the fact that our government is exercising an unusual degree of secrecy in most areas that relate to the threat of terrorism. Overall, in fact, there is a general sense that the federal government is far more secretive now than it has been for decades.

The reasons for this reticence may be easy to understand, but they also should give us pause. Much of what we know about the effectiveness of institutions—businesses, nonprofits, and especially government—suggests that good performance, over the long haul, depends on transparency and accountability. To those running such institutions, it is easy to embrace the apparent short-term advantages that flow from not having to address outside criticisms. These positive features, however, are almost always overtaken by the inevitable weaknesses that result from bureaucratic inertia and the pursuit of self-interest. Whether one is talking of Enron's mismanagement, the American Catholic Church, or the Nixon White House, it is certainly arguable that the worst problems those institutions encountered would have been reduced had there been broad and early access to emerging problems. The environment of secrecy since September 11 at the very least facilitated the systemic failures leading to the post–September 11 abuses of Muslims detained in the United States after the terrorist attacks, as well as the use of torture in American-run prisons in Iraq and Guantanamo Bay.

This year, there is an opportunity to learn a great deal more about how the government has implemented the Patriot Act, the highly controversial legislation enacted just six weeks after September 11 that transformed domestic intelligence gathering and law enforcement. Many provisions of the act are up for renewal in 2005, and the Bush administration has proposed permanently retaining all of the original bill while adding new rules as well. In the months ahead, Congress will be convening hearings connected to the act's renewal and possible expansion, which should trigger heightened media attention to its impact to date.

To help frame that debate, The Century Foundation asked New York University law professor Stephen J. Schulhofer to synthesize whatever public information has become available up to this point about how the Patriot Act has been implemented. Schulhofer is the author of *The Enemy Within: Intelligence Gathering, Law Enforcement, and Civil Liberties in the Wake of September 11*, the 2002 Century Foundation report that explained in detail the various elements of the Patriot Act while assessing its strengths and weaknesses in the battle to prevent terrorism without unnecessarily encroaching on civil liberties.

In this sequel, Schulhofer argues that while the bulk of the Patriot Act is constructive, a number of significant defects have become increasingly evident. One problem he highlights is that many of the new surveillance powers are much more extensive than necessary, with only a remote connection, at best, to preventing terrorism. It is telling that when the Justice Department has provided lists of arrests and prosecutions made possible by the Patriot Act only a few of those cases have been related to terrorism.

Another major concern, Schulhofer argues, is that the law does not provide sufficient accountability for overseeing how the new powers are carried out. Indeed, the act's limited requirements for public transparency have the potential to undercut the process of conducting a legitimate review of its impact during the renewal process. In the absence of detailed information about the implementation of the Patriot Act, the presumption that no news is good news does not serve the public interest.

This report is financed in part by a grant from the John S. and James L. Knight Foundation, which has been instrumental in the years since the September 11 attacks in enabling The Century Foundation to sponsor a wide range of activities and publications connected to homeland security. Our efforts in this area also have received substantial support from a number of other groups as well, most notably the John D. and Catherine T. MacArthur Foundation, the Robert Wood Johnson Foundation, and the Carnegie Corporation of New York. For example, with the support of the Robert Wood Johnson Foundation, we set up a working group on bioterrorism preparedness, which has resulted in the publication of a number of white papers and reports, including *Breathing Easier?* the report of the group.

In the years since the attacks, we have released many books related to homeland security issues, including *Defeating the Jihadists: A Blueprint for Action,* the report of a task force assembled and chaired by Richard A. Clarke; *War on Our Freedoms: Civil Liberties in an Age of Terrorism,* edited by Richard C. Leone and Greg Anrig, Jr.; a volume in our Basics series: *The USA Patriot Act; The Department of Homeland Security's First Year: A Report Card,* edited by Donald F. Kettl; and *A Little Knowledge: Privacy, Security, and Public Information after September 11* by Peter M. Shane, John Podesta, and Richard C. Leone, a volume cosponsored by Carnegie Mellon University's Heinz School and the Georgetown University Law Center.

We also have published many white papers examining the issues involved in homeland security since September 11, including Patricia Thomas's "The Anthrax Attacks," Elin Gursky's "Progress and Peril: Bioterrorism Preparedness Dollars and Public Health," Paula DiPerna's "Media, Charity, and Philanthropy in the Aftermath of September 11, 2001," and "Establishing a Stable Democratic Constitutional Structure in Iraq: Some Basic Considerations," which was prepared in conjunction with the Public International Law & Policy Group.

In addition, we have established a Web site, www.homelandsec.org, devoted to homeland security issues and have released numerous issue brief and papers on the subject online.

The Patriot Act was enacted in the frenzied aftermath of September 11 and in the midst of the anthrax attacks. It was understandable that Congress responded with a sense of urgency in order to demonstrate to rattled constituents that it would not be passive during that time of crisis. But there is now no excuse for failing to deliberate much more methodically over the future of this critically important law. We thank Stephen Schulhofer for producing a report that provides a valuable platform for enabling all of us to participate in those deliberations.

RICHARD C. LEONE, *President*
The Century Foundation
April 2005

CONTENTS

ACKNOWLEDGMENTS

The author wishes to acknowledge the excellent research assistance of New York University law students Chad Atlas, Erin Dow, Alex Guerrero, Amanda Lockshin, Gina Spiegelman, David Shanies, and Deepa Varma.

Chapter 1

INTRODUCTION

One of the most controversial and possibly one of the most misunderstood laws Congress ever enacted, the USA Patriot Act remains at the forefront of public debate about security and civil liberties in twenty-first-century America. For many Americans, it is synonymous with an egregious and unjustifiable suspension of the Bill of Rights. Others, troubled but more cautious, identify the Patriot Act with the grant of unprecedented powers that put civil liberties at some risk. Many who reject these concerns nonetheless accept their underlying assumption—that the Patriot Act does indeed give the federal government a package of powerful new search and surveillance tools. The 9/11 Commission unanimously agreed on a host of controversial assessments and proposals for reform, but the only conclusion it was able to reach on this subject was that "a full and informed debate on the Patriot Act would be healthy."[1]

That debate is now timely and imperative. The law's hasty enactment, in an atmosphere of trauma and urgency, virtually guaranteed serious imperfections. The passage of three years has afforded space for reflection, along with actual experience living and working with its new powers. And because many of its provisions "sunset" automatically at the end of 2005, reexamination of the act is now unavoidable for both its opponents and its most ardent defenders.

To provide a context for that reexamination, this report explains the law's most important provisions and reviews the best information currently available to gauge their usefulness and their effects in practice. This background can provide a basis for informed discussion, free of the passions and preconceptions that mere mention of the act so often evokes on all sides.

Contrary to conventional wisdom, much of the Patriot Act was essential, and some of it, if not essential, was reasonably defensible. Nonetheless, many of the act's new powers are far too broad. And even where the case for broad powers is strong, they were typically conferred with little effort to assure transparency and accountability.

These flaws are serious. Although the act's provisions often seem technical, the issues are not. Secret "sneak-and-peek" searches, computer software that reads staggering volumes of e-mail, FBI scrutiny of college transcripts and library borrowing records without probable cause, electronic surveillance under the auspices of a secretive Foreign Intelligence Surveillance Court—these are all matters that everyone can understand. They can be sources of either anxiety or reassurance: many instinctively see them as threats to liberty, while for others they promise essential protection from foreign enemies who endanger our way of life. Sometimes both reactions are justified; sometimes neither is. All too often, the act's sweeping but ill-advised new powers undermine both freedom *and* security.

To keep these concerns in perspective, it is important to acknowledge the places where the Patriot Act deserves high marks. Whatever its defects, it is more complex and more protective of basic liberty than many of its detractors acknowledge. Despite its reputation as a landmark of heightened law enforcement power, it includes provisions—seldom noticed—that add new protection for certain civil liberties, extend new benefits to certain immigrant groups, and provide new remedies for violations of individual rights. In some instances, it actually *constrains* new government powers, hedging them with thoughtfully designed safeguards. And, responding to technological changes that had outstripped an aging legal framework, the act achieves many well-justified improvements in government's ability to gather previously inaccessible information.

The flaws, however, are basic. They threaten fundamental liberties, needlessly expand dangerous powers, and in practice interfere with effective measures to thwart terrorism. We can and must do better.

THE PATRIOT ACT IN A NUTSHELL

Less than a week after the September 11 attacks, lawyers in the Department of Justice produced a voluminous draft of the legislation that was destined to become the USA Patriot Act.[2] The draft bill, running to several hundred pages, was introduced in the House of Representatives on September 19, and five days later Attorney General John Ashcroft appeared before the House Committee on the Judiciary to testify in support of it. After a truncated process of hearings in both houses and without the usual committee reports to explain it, the legislation passed by a lopsided vote in the House (357 to 66) on October 24 and by an even wider margin (98 to 1) in the Senate the next day.[3] Less than seven weeks after the attacks, on October 26, 2001, President Bush signed the measure into law.

Officially entitled the "Uniting and Strengthening America by Providing Appropriate Tools Required to Intercept and Obstruct Terrorism Act of 2001,"[4] the USA Patriot Act is widely equated— for better or worse—with the grant of exceptionally potent search and surveillance powers. That near-universal view describes, at most, only a small part of the act. The legislation is a complex grab bag of provisions addressing dozens of issues. It covers sixteen broad topics, includes 161 separate sections (most with many subsections), and fills some 350 densely printed pages. Yet, for all that it encompasses, the act is *not* the source of many of the controversial law enforcement powers sometimes associated with it. The "Patriot Act" label has often been used as a catchall for perceived overreaching by Attorney General Ashcroft or the Bush administration, but the act is *not* the basis for the administration's asserted power to hold alleged "enemy combatants" incommunicado, its assertion of the power to detain foreign nationals for long periods without filing immigration charges, or its insistence on imposing blanket orders of secrecy governing detention and hearings in immigration cases.

Among the subjects that the Patriot Act does cover, those addressed in its Title II (captioned "Enhanced Surveillance Procedures") are the ones that come immediately to mind. But the statute also includes rarely mentioned provisions that actually reduce law enforcement power and enhance civil liberties. True, there are not many of these, but they should not be overlooked.

For example, the Patriot Act took effect at a time when the Department of Justice was in its sixth week of holding hundreds of foreign nationals in secret detention without charges or hearings. The act mandated that every alien detained as a terrorist suspect must be charged within seven days or, if not, "the Attorney General shall release the alien."[5] The Justice Department subsequently ignored that restrictive portion of the statute and claimed that its own regulations

gave it an independent basis on which to continue holding the suspects without charges.[6]

The Patriot Act also suspended ordinary immigration rules and
granted special protection against deportation for surviving relatives
of foreign nationals killed on September 11.[7] Similarly, it granted a
protected immigration status to foreign nationals who were facing
deportation because they had lost their jobs as a result of the attacks.[8]

In addition to these rare liberty-enhancing provisions, the Patriot
Act covers many uncontroversial matters that are important for law
enforcement but have little or no impact on civil liberties. It provides enhanced funding for such needs as paying overtime to border
guards, upgrading visa databases and FBI computer systems, hiring
more translators, compensating the victims of September 11, and
offering rewards for those who help locate wanted terrorists.[9] It
includes measures to improve training programs for intelligence officers, coordination between the CIA and the FBI, and collaboration
among federal, state, and local law enforcement.[10] Another provision
governs the licensing of drivers who transport hazardous materi-
als.[11] The act creates a new agency to study and reduce the vulnera-
bility of "critical infrastructure," such as ports, power plants, and
chemical factories.[12]

More controversially, the legislation changes the definition of
some terrorism offenses, and it increases the punishments applicable
to those convicted of certain terrorist crimes.[13] One section expands
the scope of the offense of providing "material support" to a terrorist organization, in language that at least one federal court has held
unconstitutionally vague.[14]

Some parts of the Patriot Act have only tenuous connections to
fighting terrorism. One, for example, grants increased funding to
train the Drug Enforcement Agency operatives who combat opium
production in Central Asia.[15]

Among the provisions that do affect the fight against terrorism,
many also are relevant to broader problems, including deportation,
procedures for processing visa applications, and the monitoring of
foreign nationals studying in the United States.[16] Similarly, the extensive sections covering banking, financial regulations, and international money laundering[17] have obvious value for monitoring terrorist
activity and choking off its sources of funds, but these measures were
designed to be available for other purposes as well. Indeed, many of
them are primarily used to deal with criminal, administrative, and

regulatory matters not related to terrorism.[18] In most of these areas, the enhanced governmental powers conferred by the Patriot Act pose significant problems—potential government overreaching, inefficiency, and abuse—even when they do not implicate core First Amendment freedoms and Fourth Amendment privacy rights.

Several important layers of related powers and restrictions flow from the Intelligence Reform Act of 2004.[19] This statute is principally concerned with the reorganization of the intelligence community and the creation of a new "czar," the director of national intelligence, to oversee the intelligence operations of the Central Intelligence Agency, the Pentagon, and other agencies. In addition, however, it modifies many of the laws and regulations identified with the Patriot Act. It expands the scope of foreign intelligence surveillance,[20] tightens the money-laundering laws,[21] and strengthens the power to detain suspected terrorists prior to trial.[22] It sets minimum federal standards for personal identity documents and attempts to bolster their security.[23] It clarifies (and enlarges) the crime of providing "material support" to a terrorist organization, but it also limits the scope of the offense to those who have actual knowledge of the organization's terrorist character.[24] Finally, it creates a Privacy and Civil Liberties Oversight Board in the Executive Office of the President and sets up offices in the Department of Homeland Security charged with ensuring that the department's policies and procedures adequately safeguard privacy, civil rights, and civil liberties.[25]

In rethinking the Patriot Act, this report will make no effort to discuss all these subjects comprehensively. Instead, it focuses on the statutory sections with the most direct implications for civil liberties, specifically the provisions of Title II that bolster the government's intelligence-gathering authority, along with closely related provisions scattered elsewhere throughout the Patriot Act and the 2004 Intelligence Reform Act.

Title II covers in several dozen sections and subsections a wide array of important and controversial topics. Though daunting in their detail and technical complexity, these measures fall into several broad groups. Of twenty-seven distinct provisions addressing search and surveillance matters, four deal exclusively with mechanics (translators, the number of judges, and compensation for expenses incurred by private communications firms).[26] Five expand search and surveillance powers applicable only to foreign intelligence and international terrorism investigations.[27] Another of the foreign intelligence provisions concerns government access to previously private records, such as business documents, medical histories, and library borrowings.[28] The remaining seventeen provisions are all concerned with conventional law enforcement powers.[29] The new measures in this last group are available not only for international terrorism investigations but also for the investigation of purely domestic crimes, even those not in any way related to terrorism.

GRAVE DEFECTS

Although the Patriot Act achieves many needed improvements in government's intelligence-gathering capabilities, its defects are pervasive, tainting large numbers of otherwise disparate provisions.

First, it confers many surveillance powers that are broader than necessary. Some have only a remote connection to the battle against terrorism. Some have no relationship whatever to the terror threat. FBI and Treasury agents can use most of their new powers to investigate allegations of prostitution, gambling, insider trading, or any other offense.

Second, the new powers, even where justified, are seldom accompanied by guarantees of transparency or measures to preserve checks and balances. Of course, some secrecy and some degree of executive independence is a necessity in law enforcement, particularly when confronting an organization like al Qaeda. But throughout the act, accountability was diluted unnecessarily; in some instances accountability measures previously taken for granted were obliterated.

Third, the pervasive absence of adequate structures of accountability is no minor detail. This flaw is dangerous. It exacts a large price in lost liberty and heightens the risk of governmental abuse; that much is obvious. Less obvious, but for some citizens possibly more important, the absence of adequate accountability undermines the counterterrorism campaign itself.

Insufficient transparency and accountability inevitably produce waste and misdirected effort. What is far worse, government puts its own legitimacy at risk. As law enforcement and surveillance powers grow in times like the present, there is ever-increasing danger that suspicion of government—whether justified or not—will grow along with it, canceling many of the gains that Congress hoped the enhanced powers would achieve.

Essential Remedies

In attempting to sort through a dense thicket of distinct problems to be solved, this report will suggest two deceptively simple but pervasively useful rules of thumb. First, in responding to extraordinary threats to our security, we must ensure that the extraordinary powers we grant are *narrowly tailored*. Second, we must take care to guarantee *maximum feasible accountability.*

Narrow Tailoring

Many of the new Patriot Act powers are exceptionally wide-ranging. Most Americans already understand that and are not particularly alarmed. What would be alarming for many people would be for the government *not* to err in the direction of deploying strong law enforcement powers.

Nonetheless, a close, critical look at these measures is imperative, and not only for the familiar reason that civil liberties are too easily devalued. Talk of a "trade-off" between liberty and security implies that decreases in liberty produce at least some increase in security, but too often overbroad law enforcement powers backfire. Since September 11, that dynamic has led us to sacrifice important liberties unnecessarily while at the same time undermining our security.

Accountability

Whatever the urgency, following September 11, to reposition the line between law enforcement power and individual rights, this imperative does not in itself imply a need to suspend the mechanisms of accountability that traditionally frame executive power, even in wartime. If anything, there is need, as investigative powers expand, for stronger and more effective oversight. As the 9/11 Commission's unanimous report noted:[30] "The American public has vested enormous authority in the U.S. government. . . . This shift of power and authority to the government calls for an *enhanced* system of checks and balances to protect the precious liberties that are vital to our way of life."

Secrecy and the absence of accountability are troublesome, and not just because they risk unnecessary invasions of liberty and privacy. They also are a recipe for wasted effort, misdirected resources, and misuse of legitimately acquired information for illegitimate purposes.

This is not a partisan concern. Its force does not depend on whether the nation's attorney general is Janet Reno, John Ashcroft, or Alberto Gonzales. Suspicion of unchecked executive power began with the administration of George Washington, probably the most widely trusted leader in our history, and it has been the lesson of experience in every other country around the world.

Understandably, the Justice Department has been frustrated by the documentation and justification that accountability invariably entails. It has sometimes explained the need to reduce the judicial role on the ground that resources consumed by administrative requirements could better be devoted to investigative effort on the ground.[31] Again, the universal experience is that well-designed checks and balances, though they seem cumbersome, invariably pay their way. The solution to the dilemma is not to stint on investigation; nor is it to sacrifice the rule of law in order to free personnel for field work. Instead, it is simply to commit the modest resources required for appropriate documentation, accountability, and oversight. Facing threats and resource constraints at least as serious as those the United States confronts, the Israeli supreme court recently reaffirmed that difficulty in organizing sufficient personnel to permit effective judicial review cannot justify curtailment of checks and balances. Rather, the court stressed, when "emergency conditions undoubtedly demanded a large-scale deployment of forces . . . by the same standards, effort and resources must be invested in the protection of the detainees' rights."[32]

The unusual challenges of a war on terrorism in no way diminish the traditional importance of accountability. On the contrary, the superficial attractions of unchecked executive power are especially deceptive and shortsighted in today's world. Our security depends on building confidence, here and around the globe, not only that America is strong but that America is fair, a society in which our government practices what it preaches in terms of human rights, treats all people with decency, and respects the rule of law.

If we fear potential terrorists lurking in our communities of Muslim Americans and immigrants from the Middle East, we will do far better to work at winning the respect and cooperation of law abiding members of those communities than to alienate them by oppressive surveillance and harsh policies of detention and deportation. Yet, the current acceptance of secrecy and unchecked law enforcement power sows alienation and mistrust. With their penchant for secrecy, their strong preference for unilateral executive power, their disdain for international human rights, and their efforts to detain Muslim citizens and foreign nationals with no access to lawyers or to the courts, America's present policies pursue short-term gain (usually slender at best) at the price of fostering lasting animosity and resentment among the very people here and abroad whose help we need most to break the cycle of terrorist violence.

This report examines the Patriot Act closely with these concerns in mind. Before plunging into the statutory details, however, it is essential to consider the nature of the terrorist challenge and to assess the importance of more powerful surveillance tools in the effort to meet it—their value, their limitations, and the risks they pose, not only to civil liberties but to the success of the counterterrorism campaign itself.

Chapter 2

UNDERSTANDING THE CHALLENGE
SURVEILLANCE NEEDS AND
THEIR DANGERS

Anyone seeking to assess the Patriot Act must first understand the threats our nation faces and its deficiencies in confronting them. Nothing could be clearer than the indelible image of the burning towers. But that picture is not sufficient to define the problem. What specific weaknesses enabled the September 11 plot to succeed, and what steps are necessary to minimize the risk of future attacks? Is the struggle against terrorism a "war," and, if so, what weapons should be used to fight it? Can restrictions on individual liberty help in identifying, locating, and ultimately thwarting terrorists?

A "WAR" ON TERRORISM?

In practical terms, it may not matter greatly whether one chooses to label the present challenge a war. But labels have a way of shaping responses, for better or worse.

In declaring a "war" on terrorism, the president underscored the gravity of the danger, the urgency of a nationwide mobilization of thinking and resources, and the need to attack al Qaeda's overseas bases with military force, including both targeted special operations and conventional combat against the armed forces of the Taliban government in Afghanistan. These legitimate concerns, all enjoying broad public support, created a situation with little resemblance to ordinary law enforcement or mobilization to confront social challenges. This is no "war on drugs" or "war on poverty."

But this situation, a genuine war, is far removed from domestic intelligence gathering and other responses within our own borders. It does not by itself mean that this country should militarize the protective steps we take at home. And even if we decided to do that, the situation would not for that reason justify complete deference to the president or suspension of the Bill of Rights.

Despite widespread misunderstanding and misrepresentation of this point in the general media, wartime presidents have never been granted complete deference, even in situations of total mobilization (World War II) or large-scale combat on our own soil (the Civil War). Neither the first Gulf War, the Korean War, nor the Vietnam War (the latter lasting nearly a decade) was accompanied by any important increase in presidential prerogatives. None of these recent wars was thought to call for restraining the level of political criticism or the reach of the Bill of Rights. In rejecting Bush administration claims of executive power to detain citizens indefinitely with no judicial review, the Supreme Court recently reaffirmed this long-settled point: "A state of war is not a blank check for the President when it comes to the rights of the Nation's citizens."[1] The language of "war" may pay political dividends for the administration in power, especially if the public does not understand past wartime practice, but being at war does not automatically change the civil liberties equation.

The war framework does make a difference, however, in its potential to distort our choices of domestic policies and strategies. When transferred from military operations in Afghanistan to the context of intelligence gathering and other measures deployed within our borders, the classic military model—troops, tanks, airstrikes, and house-to-house searches—is obviously inappropriate. But that fact does not mean that the conventional law enforcement model is the appropriate one, either. To be sure, al Qaeda bears some similarity to a large and particularly lethal criminal conspiracy, a major drug cartel or international racketeering enterprise. But one difference has overriding practical significance.

Conventional law enforcement is predominantly retrospective. Though it can sometimes interrupt a conspiracy in the making, its primary goal is to exact retribution and deter future offenses by capturing and punishing those who have already perpetrated a crime. In confronting the terror tactics of modern Islamic extremists, that approach will not do. Al Qaeda operatives often have no expectation (or desire) to survive a successful attack. Once such an attack occurs, retribution and deterrence by capture and punishment of the perpetrator are no longer relevant options. And, even when available, such measures are painfully inadequate. For conventional crimes, even for such serious crimes as murder and rape, it is normally *after* the offense that society expects investigators to spring into action, assembling clues and working back from evidence at the crime scene to identify, prosecute, convict, and punish the perpetrator. But modern terror attacks, with their catastrophic loss of life and staggering economic impact, must be stopped before they occur.

This contrast has pervasive practical consequences. No matter how widespread or brutal it may be, a drug cartel or organized crime syndicate can be fought with tactics that remain predominantly retrospective and punitive. Investigators can work back from evidence at a crime scene to identify and prosecute the perpetrator. And they can then enlist that person's cooperation in identifying those higher up. But when preventive goals dominate, the universe of information to be collected, sifted, and interpreted is infinitely wider. The need to work with multiple teams on diverse assignments grows exponentially. Paperwork, administrative approvals, and other delays impose more serious costs; everything must be done quickly, in real time. War is not a good way to describe such a process, but, unlike the "war on drugs," it cannot simply be redescribed as conventional law enforcement.

Whatever may be the diplomatic and military measures that we deploy overseas, government agencies must do what they can domestically to protect against the ongoing threat from al Qaeda and from the wider domain of radical global terrorist movements. This must be, above all else, a proactive and preventive effort.

THE NEED FOR STRONGER LEGAL TOOLS

Well-designed legal powers play a vital role in facilitating vigorous, proactive strategies and successful preventive efforts. Legal authority can be the key to obtaining essential information about adversaries and their unfolding plans. But we must not overestimate the significance of law, even such a comprehensive and important law as the Patriot Act.

The value of access to more and better information seems self-evident—so self-evident that many Americans now think it prudent to give counterterrorism officials broad authority to collect whatever information they consider useful. This widely shared assumption is not, at first blush, unreasonable. But it is misleading because legal authority is much less important for successful intelligence operations than the public and the legal profession generally believe.

An effective intelligence process requires that information be gathered, translated (when necessary), pooled by the relevant agencies, analyzed, and then transmitted to those in a position to investigate further or take quick preventive action. Legal rules are largely irrelevant at the crucial stages of translation, analysis, and transmission. Law can pose significant hurdles to the pooling of intelligence, but here the obstacles of agency culture, cumbersome lines of communication, and limited resources usually matter much more. Even at the stage of gathering domestic intelligence, the stage where we expect law to govern, capabilities are largely determined by nonlegal constraints: technical, budgetary, and human resources, the training and priorities of officers, and the organization and cultures of the relevant agencies.

If an intelligence process suffers from major deficits in these areas, preoccupation with questions of legal authority can be a dangerous distraction because it will inevitably prevent us from addressing problems that may matter much more. Before focusing on the legal issues in detail, it is essential to assess the role they played in the events leading up to the September 11 attacks.

INTELLIGENCE-GATHERING EFFORTS PRIOR TO SEPTEMBER 11

In the first weeks after September 11, 2001, it was widely assumed that our intelligence agencies had been denied the use of legal tools that could have provided warning of terrorist plans. Commentators endlessly repeated the supposed truism that the attacks demonstrated the need to "shift the balance" between liberty and security. Decreasing our liberty, the cliché implied, would give us increased security.

The proposals eventually embodied in the Patriot Act reflect that assumption. They draw attention, over and over, to areas where the

Justice Department lacked various sorts of investigative power. That emphasis, whatever its purpose, had the effect of deflecting attention from questions about what the FBI could have done and should have done with the powers already at its disposal. Indeed, the very process of putting forward the Patriot Act remedies and pressing for their rapid enactment reinforced the implicit diagnosis that the public and most pundits had quickly reached in any event—that legal restrictions and measures meant to safeguard civil liberties were in substantial measure to blame for the intelligence failures of September 11.

The truth, as is now known, was far different. Before September 11, the government possessed far-reaching intelligence-gathering authority, including broad electronic surveillance powers and still broader search and surveillance authorities available under the Foreign Intelligence Surveillance Act (FISA). And FISA authority, though primarily concerned with monitoring agents of foreign governments, also was available for monitoring individuals (both foreign nationals and U.S. citizens) believed to be associated with international terrorism, even when they were not affiliated with any foreign government. FISA had been used frequently for just that purpose.

Though the available legal powers were not unlimited, it has become clear that legal limitations bear little if any of the blame for the failure to prevent September 11. Rather, severe budgetary and organizational deficits, together with inexplicable human blunders, prevented law enforcement and intelligence agencies from using their strong legal powers effectively. Bipartisan examinations of the events by a joint congressional inquiry and by the 9/11 Commission came to the same, unanimous conclusion on this point.

Nor is this simply a matter of twenty-twenty hindsight. A detailed FBI assessment of its counterterrorism capabilities, the "Director's Report on Terrorism," was ordered toward the end of the Clinton administration and completed in the spring of 2001. The report found numerous weaknesses and made extensive recommendations, focusing not on legal restrictions but rather on shortfalls in available personnel, organization, computer quality, and analytic capabilities.[2] It stressed above all that a productive counterterrorism effort required more budgetary support. Yet, on September 10, in a political environment that gave high priority to shrinking "big government," Attorney General John Ashcroft rejected an FBI request for an additional $58 million to strengthen its counterterrorism effort.[3]

To be sure, there were legal weaknesses as well. Rules that restricted the sharing of grand jury and FISA information, in the interest of preserving secrecy, privacy, and accountability, no longer took adequate account of the need for wider dissemination of such information within the law enforcement and intelligence communities. Paradoxically, one result of the growing interpenetration of the law-enforcement and foreign-intelligence functions was an increasingly elaborate system of regulations designed to keep them confined to separate spheres, an effort that made appropriate use of the FISA process more difficult than the law actually required. Layered on top of these regulations were a variety of other bureaucratic roadblocks, agency traditions, and purely technological barriers, all impeding communication and cooperation within the government. (For more detailed discussion of these problems, see Chapter 3.)

Compounding these difficulties were egregious FBI management failures, most of which were well known within the Bureau for years before September 11. As detailed by the Leahy-Grassley-Specter report for the Senate Judiciary Committee,[4] a cumbersome and stodgy FBI bureaucracy habitually stifled the initiative of agents in the field. Bureau managers controlling crucial steps in the warrant application process did not know what the relevant legal standards were and imagined legal requirements that did not exist.[5] More senior managers noticed grave deficiencies in agents' understanding of the law but did nothing to address the problem. When managers at headquarters did try to lend assistance, they were often stymied by a computer system that made it difficult to access and cross-reference information.[6]

A General Accounting Office audit released in July 2001 attempted to draw public attention to these problems and expressed concern over the continued delays in rectifying them. The report's title tells the story: "Coordination within Justice on Counterintelligence Criminal Matters Is Limited."[7] Among other problems, FBI agents and staff lawyers in the Justice Department's Office of Intelligence Policy and Review (OIPR) were overly cautious in their interpretation of surveillance requirements, and senior officials felt that the staff lawyers were blocking legitimate investigative efforts.[8] The problem was one of approach rather than the statutory requirements themselves; yet the GAO report indicates that little was being done to correct it. Moreover, staff attorneys had alerted senior officials to a serious personnel bottleneck: with heightened attention to terrorism, FBI requests for FISA surveillance warrants had increased significantly during the preceding years, but "OIPR resources needed to process those requests had not kept apace."[9]

Long before the GAO audit, Justice Department lawyers concerned about these problems had formed a working group to address them. The working group's memorandum, with recommended solutions, had been submitted to the attorney general's office for decision in late 2000. Yet, as of July 2001, no decision on the memorandum had been made.[10] Responding to GAO's concerns about inaction, Justice Department officials suggested in their defense that the issue was sensitive and difficult, one that "the Attorney General continues to review."[11] This did not satisfy GAO auditors, who noted presciently:

> This issue has been longstanding and the concerns that it has generated by some officials [have] inhibited the [goal] to ensure that DOJ's criminal and counterintelligence functions were properly coordinated. Because such coordination can be critical to the successful achievement of both counterintelligence investigations and criminal prosecutions, *the issue needs to be resolved as soon as possible.* We remain concerned that *delays in resolving these issues could have serious adverse effects on critical cases involving national security issues.*[12]

These systemic problems all took their toll on specific investigative steps during the run-up to September 11. FBI agents and other officials began to receive information that raised bright red flags about the unfolding plot. By the summer of 2001 intelligence agents were aware that something big was afoot, though many believed that U.S. interests overseas were the most likely target. An intelligence memo distributed in late June indicated a high probability of "spectacular" terrorist attacks in the near future,[13] and CIA director George Tenet recalled that by July "the system was blinking red."[14] Agents also knew that several dangerous al Qaeda operatives (two of the eventual hijackers) had entered the United States but did not grasp the significance of their travel patterns. And not until August 2001 did agents launch an effort to locate them.

The stumbling block to uncovering the September 11 plot or intercepting these hijackers therefore was not a lack of surveillance authority or even a failure to pick up the telltale facts. Rather, it was the failure to understand the information already gathered, a failure that was in part the product of FBI and CIA unwillingness to share leads within and between their agencies. As one FBI agent put it, "We didn't know what we knew."[15]

The failures to pool and relay intelligence were almost exclusively attributable not to legal obstacles but to agency cultures, poor training, and obsolete lines of communication. Rules that barred law enforcement officials from sharing grand jury information, for example, played no role in impeding preventive action prior to September 11. There was no secret grand jury material that would, if disseminated, have alerted counterterrorism units or provided more dots for them to connect. There existed a considerable amount of alarming information on the law enforcement side as a result of the East African embassy and 1993 World Trade Center bombing investigations. This information, however, was part of the trial record in those cases and was readily available to officials outside law enforcement and indeed to the general public.[16]

Among the most frustrating parts of the September 11 story are the repeated instances in which agents did obtain highly revealing information but failed to pass it along to others who would have been in a position to connect the dots. The episodes are recounted in detail and analyzed in the 9/11 Commission's report. Once again, legal walls did not cause these failures of communication. One telling instance, on June 11, 2001, was all too typical. An FBI agent (identified as "Jane") and a CIA analyst (identified as "Dave") met in New York with FBI agents working on the investigation into the bombing of the destroyer *Cole*. They brought with them photographs of suspected al Qaeda operatives they had been attempting to trace, in order to see if the New York agents recognized any of them. The New York agents were anxious to know where the photos had been taken and why—information that, if conveyed, would have pointed to alarming ties between al Qaeda and several subjects of their own investigation. But "Jane" mistakenly believed that she could not tell the New York agents what she knew. Moreover, the New York agents never put their questions to "Dave," and he simply chose not to volunteer anything.[17]

Later that summer, "Jane" again failed to pass along critical information that could have helped an FBI criminal investigator who was looking for one of the eventual hijackers. As the 9/11 Commission concluded, "Simply put, there was no legal reason why the information the analyst possessed could not have been shared with the criminal agent."[18]

The joint congressional inquiry and the 9/11 Commission's report document similar alarm bells that were repeatedly ignored by others who were in a position to take investigative action. Even in the summer of 2001, with growing indications of a serious threat environment, there was little investigative focus on the would-be hijackers or their accomplices. There was virtually no effort to deploy readily available investigative tools to gather more information about them. Grave nonlegal deficiencies—in organization, staffing levels, technical resources, competence, and priority setting—cost our security watchdogs what chances they had to abort the plot.

The now familiar flight school alerts in July and August 2001 are worth special attention in this regard because some public commentators have incorrectly attributed inaction on those matters to perceived legal constraints.

THE PHOENIX FIELD OFFICE REQUEST

In July 2001 officials at FBI headquarters and elsewhere ignored a Phoenix field office request for an investigation of suspicious individuals seeking flight training. Testimony before the 9/11 Commission and the joint congressional inquiry does not identify any specific reason for FBI inaction at that crucial juncture; it seems possible that no FBI official made a conscious decision on the matter at all. Some public reports cite a lack of sufficient resources to pursue the field office request; others refer to a purported concern to avoid conducting operations that might be perceived as "racial profiling." Whatever the explanation, the Bureau unquestionably had ample legal authority to pursue such an investigation.

THE MOUSSAOUI SEARCH REQUEST

The Bureau's handling of Zacarias Moussaoui, one of the tragic errors in the months leading up to September 11, dramatically illustrates failures that were rooted almost exclusively in budget constraints, organizational weaknesses, and poor training.[19] After Moussaoui's arrest in August 2001, the Minneapolis field office asked headquarters to seek a warrant to search his computer and other personal effects. (After September 11, when that search was finally conducted, it turned up leads that might—though no one can be sure—have led to the arrest of one or more hijackers.) A supervisor in the counterterrorism unit rejected the August request, informing agent Coleen Rowley that more information was necessary. Precious days were lost while Rowley attempted to assemble additional details that the law did not require. Yet, the supervisor at headquarters did not check his own database for leads concerning suspicious use of American flight schools, a step that might have led him to the alarming report filed by the Phoenix field office just a month before.

In short, time pressure, resource constraints, grossly deficient training, and a culture of caution (and indeed obstruction) prevented agents from availing themselves of strong, readily available powers. And the failure to search Moussaoui's computer and personal effects was not an isolated incident. It appears that a pattern of missteps continued for many critical months when existing tools, properly used, might have made a difference.

Assessing the Pre–September 11 Powers

The adequacy of the FBI's legal powers prior to September 11 is not open to doubt or debate. Both the public record and the assessments based on classified information made available to the 9/11 Commission and the joint congressional inquiry make clear that the law enforcement and intelligence communities had strong domestic intelligence-gathering powers that were not deployed effectively even when alarming indications of an unfolding terrorist threat were in hand. There is little doubt that broader authority likewise would have remained unused because inadequacies in human, budgetary, and organizational resources, compounded in some instances by incompetence, prevented the effective use of whatever legal tools would have been available.

The 9/11 Commission's conclusions are emphatic on these points:

> [FBI Director Louis] Freeh recognized terrorism as a major threat.
> . . . Freeh's efforts did not, however, translate into a significant
> shift of resources to counterterrorism. [A 1998] five-year strategic
> plan . . . did not obtain the necessary human resources. . . . FBI
> counterterrorism spending remained fairly constant between fiscal

years 1998 and 2001. In 2000 there were still twice as many agents devoted to drug enforcement as to counterterrorism.

Second, the new division intended to strengthen the FBI's strategic analysis capability faltered. It received insufficient resources and faced resistance from senior managers. . . . Analysts continued to be used in a tactical [not analytic] fashion. . . .

Moreover, analysts had difficulty getting access to the FBI and intelligence community information they were expected to analyze. The poor state of the FBI's information systems meant that such access depended in large part on an analyst's personal relationships. . . .

Third, the FBI did not have an effective intelligence collection effort. Collection of intelligence from human sources was limited, and agents were inadequately trained. . . . The FBI did not dedicate sufficient resources to the surveillance and translation needs of counterterrorism agents. It lacked sufficient translators proficient in Arabic and other key languages, resulting in a significant backlog of untranslated intercepts.

Finally, the FBI's information systems were woefully inadequate. The FBI lacked the ability to know what it knew: There was no effective mechanism for capturing or sharing its institutional knowledge.[20]

In the wake of the attacks, however, the Justice Department's push to enact the Patriot Act served to divert attention from these grave shortcomings, most of which were firmly established on the record well before September 11. The act's long list of ostensibly needed statutory amendments served to point a finger of blame at the laws on the books: "safeguard x" and "limitation y" had precluded appropriate investigative steps. The legal framework became the focus of attention and the other—far more important—prerequisites of an efficacious counterterrorism effort disappeared from view.

LOOKING AHEAD: THE ONGOING NEED FOR STRONGER SURVEILLANCE AUTHORITY

Those who are concerned with designing tools to respond to the threat of terrorism cannot limit their attention to the role that legal constraints played in the past, of course. Legal issues that did not

matter in the run-up to September 11 could become important imped-
iments to preventing the next attack. The public would justifiably
fault the Department of Justice if it did not seek to remove legal
obstacles that could prove costly in the years ahead.

Three needs in particular stand out in the effort to adapt law
enforcement and surveillance authorities to the struggle against terrorism. First, because agents must emphasize proactive and preventive
measures, rather than the retrospective tactics of conventional law
enforcement, effective coordination between the law enforcement and
intelligence communities is essential. Compartmentalized teams and
"walls" that impede communication must be eliminated. Second, for
the same reason, speed is essential; paperwork, administrative
approvals, and delay must wherever possible be kept to a minimum.
Finally, complex statutes tailored to the specifics of the telephone
and other older technologies need updating. The law must confer
comparable surveillance powers—and comparable privacy guarantees—for newer modes of communication and for the distinctive business models being used to provide them.

At the same time, Congress must be sure to keep such concerns
in their proper perspective. There are reasons to proceed cautiously in
expanding surveillance and intelligence-gathering authorities as the
Patriot Act does.

HIDDEN COSTS OF EXPANDING
THE LEGAL ARSENAL

Before focusing on the many plausible ways to strengthen governmental surveillance authority, we must remember two caveats. First,
the overriding priority must be to fix the huge *nonlegal* deficiencies
that currently hamper efforts to gather and use information effectively. Legal problems can be fascinating, and, though often difficult,
they can be seductive because so often they seem comparatively easy
to solve; if legal authority is lacking, a new statute can fill the gap with
the stroke of a pen. Such solutions are tempting because intuition
suggests that more surveillance power will deliver immediate law
enforcement payoffs. But fascination with legal issues or the attractions of the easy fix must not divert attention and energy from more
difficult problems that in the end are infinitely more important.

Second, stronger intelligence-gathering authority not only delivers smaller benefits than expected; it also entails large, easily overlooked costs. In times of public danger and stress, the temptation is always strong to drop objective prerequisites for surveillance, to relax oversight, and to grant investigators wide discretion. But broad powers and diminished accountability are not cost-free. Americans cannot assume that it is safe simply to confer extra powers here and there for good measure.

And the possible consequences are not merely speculative. Prior to the intelligence reforms of the 1970s, the FBI held broad surveillance powers much like those that many Americans once again consider appropriate. The results are well documented.

BROAD SURVEILLANCE POWERS IN OPERATION

Faced with what was then perceived as a grave threat of Communist infiltration and subversion (Soviet agents in the United States had helped Russia acquire the secret of the atom bomb; China and the Eastern European countries had recently fallen under Communist rule), the FBI agents of the 1950s and 1960s were entrusted with a life-and-death mission and broad surveillance powers to carry it out vigorously. Free to pursue random tips and their own hunches, they intimidated dissidents, damaged the reputations of many who were not, and produced thick dossiers on politicians, other public figures, political and religious groups, and hundreds of thousands of individuals. FBI director J. Edgar Hoover did not hesitate to use the Bureau's extensive dossiers to enhance his power, silence opponents, and ensure the support of important members of Congress.

Today, many who are unaware of that history are inclined to dismiss fear of FBI misconduct as hyperbole, the complaint of the oversensitive and the radical fringe. Yet the gravity of those FBI abuses and their staggering extent were fully and conclusively documented by a 1976 bipartisan congressional panel, the Church Committee, many of whose members had begun the inquiry confidently assuming that the charges against the FBI were wildly exaggerated. In this regard, remarks made to the Church Committee by Senator Phillip Hart are especially pertinent today:

I have been told for years . . . that this [misconduct] is exactly
what the Bureau was doing all of the time, and . . . I assured them
that they were [wrong]—it just wasn't true. . . . I did not believe it.

The trick now, Mr. Chairman, is for this committee to be able
to figure out how to persuade the people of this country that
indeed it did go on. And how shall we insure that it will never
happen again? But *it will happen repeatedly unless we can bring
ourselves to understand and accept that it did go on.*[21]

The committee's findings were chilling. Agents zealously pursuing leads and hunches saw nothing wrong in showing their badge
and "just asking" employers and teachers whether an individual had
been seen with Communists, had expressed hatred of America, or
had shown a desire to commit violent acts against the government.
Agents spent years infiltrating and monitoring political groups of all
stripes, from the Socialist Workers Party on the left to the
Conservative American Christian Action Council and the John Birch
Society on the right. Attending rallies and meetings open to the public, they monitored and maintained extensive files on student groups
on college campuses, civil rights organizations including the NAACP
and the Southern Christian Leadership Conference, national leaders
such as the Rev. Martin Luther King, Jr., antiwar groups, and meetings they identified with the "Women's Liberation Movement."[22]

Investigations of the NAACP, initiated on suspicion that the
group had ties to Communists, continued for years, even though
agents reported that the NAACP strenuously avoided such ties.
Antiwar and civil rights groups were monitored on the pretext (not
always unfounded) that these groups might plan illegal marches, sit-
ins, or trespass demonstrations at civilian or military facilities. Martin
Luther King, Jr., was subjected to years of surveillance, legal and illegal, to determine whether his professed commitment to nonviolence
was a sham and to acquire personal information that could be used to
discredit him.

The Church Committee found, moreover, that "intelligence activities [tend] to expand beyond their initial scope. . . . Intelligence collection programs naturally generate ever-increasing demands for new
data. . . . [Investigations have] swept in vast amounts of information
about the personal lives, views, and associations of American citizens."[23] One agent who supported the effort to collect such intelligence nonetheless acknowledged that some investigators "would

construe political considerations to be national security considerations, [and] move from the kid with a bomb to the kid with a picket sign, and from [there] to the kid with the bumper sticker of the opposing candidate. And you just keep going down the line."[24] By 1975 FBI headquarters held in excess of half a million domestic intelligence files, most containing information on more than one individual, and there were many additional files in the field offices. In 1972 alone, the Bureau opened 65,000 new domestic intelligence files.[25]

In the name of anticipating disorder, protecting national security, and unearthing hidden links to a radical extremist movement (communism), FBI agents, sometimes with direction from Washington but often on their own initiative, damaged reputations, disrupted legitimate protest groups, and "deter[red] the exercise of First Amend[ment] rights."[26] The Bureau was quite simply out of control.

LEARNING FROM HISTORY OR REPEATING IT?

The challenge now facing our nation is to create a framework for vigorous intelligence gathering and rapid initiatives in counterterrorism matters without opening the door to the abuses of the past or their contemporary equivalents. One need not fear the appointment of a new J. Edgar Hoover to worry that broad discretion to initiate surveillance, build files, and spy on dissident political and religious minorities could harm innocent individuals, stifle First Amendment freedoms, and waste limited investigative resources that, now more than ever, need to stay targeted on the most serious potential threats. In 1972, at the height of the Vietnam War, the Supreme Court stressed these concerns in holding that executive searches in national security cases are unconstitutional unless authorized by a judicial warrant: "National security cases . . . often reflect a convergence of First and Fourth Amendment values not present in cases of 'ordinary crime.' Though the investigative duty of the executive may be stronger in such cases, so also is there greater jeopardy to constitutionally protected speech."[27]

Nor can today's field offices and individual agents be counted on to act wisely and selectively without independent oversight. An FBI field office recently courted international ridicule by spending six months wiretapping a well-known New Orleans brothel to investigate the scope of prostitution in that city.[28]

In this regard, the Church Committee's findings on the subject of "accountability and control" have particular contemporary relevance:[29]

> The overwhelming number of excesses continuing over a prolonged period of time were due in large measure to the fact that the system of checks and balances . . . was seldom applied to the intelligence community. Guidance and regulation . . . has been vague. . . . Presidents and other senior Executive officials, particularly the Attorneys General, have virtually abdicated their Constitutional responsibility to oversee and set standards for intelligence activity.

That history spotlights several distinct harms that result from conferring too much intelligence-gathering power. One of these, the loss of privacy and similar liberties, is self-evident but too often ignored. Another also is frequently forgotten. Even when government agents justifiably intrude into private domains and collect sensitive information for appropriate reasons, there remains a substantial danger that, without adequate safeguards, the information legitimately acquired will be misused for illegitimate purposes. The FBI history, unfortunately, offers far too many examples of this tendency, even in an agency largely staffed by dedicated and conscientious professionals.

Legislators often believe that by enacting strong legal powers, they can avoid the painful step of approving costly expenditures on security. But, unless they are fooling themselves (or their constituents), this approach is not a solution because intelligence-gathering powers are themselves expensive to use. Large investments in personnel and technical resources are necessary to acquire information, and additional resources are required to process information effectively. Conferring tough new legal powers without committing the resources necessary to implement them can be worse than useless. After events like those of September 11, the public insists that political leaders take action; new laws like the Patriot Act can meet that demand and thus become a substitute for the more expensive but more efficacious measures that lawmakers would otherwise be obliged to enact.

Three additional concerns are less familiar and perhaps more surprising because they involve ways in which overbroad powers hamper the law enforcement effort itself.

First, comprehensive surveillance powers, freed from the burdens of objective justification and oversight, are invariably a recipe for "mission creep," wasted resources and misdirected effort. The FBI history, again, furnishes many examples of this tendency for conscientious agents to misplace priorities and lose sight of larger goals.

Second, insufficiently selective surveillance means information overload on the front end of the intelligence process. Prior to September 11, the FBI was hobbled not by a lack of sufficient raw data to analyze but by its inability to separate significant intelligence from "noise." Under those circumstances, augmenting the stream of information flowing into FBI files will not help and may even aggravate the difficulty. Indeed, even before September 11 the Treasury Department was receiving every month more than 15,000 suspicious activity reports and more than a million currency transaction reports.[30] The problem of information overload became so acute that Congress—in the Patriot Act itself—instructed the Treasury Department to find ways to cut down on the amount of intelligence collected because the volume of reports was "interfering with effective law enforcement."[31]

Yet, the steps taken since September 11 pay little heed to this side of the intelligence-gathering equation. Recent efforts to enhance staffing, computer functions, and analytic capability[32] will mitigate the problem but not if they are counterbalanced by indiscriminate growth of raw data to be evaluated. As of September 2004, the Justice Department reported that more than 120,000 hours of surveillance tapes remained untranslated at FBI headquarters because of a continuing shortage of qualified personnel.[33] Casting an ever wider net for surveillance information will only make the job of intelligence analysts more difficult.

Finally, and most important, broad powers and diminished accountability undermine trust and impair the perceived legitimacy of the entire law enforcement effort. Even when government agents are acting in the best of faith, they risk arousing suspicion—and even resentment and hostility—on the part of law-abiding individuals who feel they may fall under the sweep of such powers. Worldwide, there are at most only a few thousand dedicated Islamic extremists determined to do harm. But there are more than one million law-abiding Muslims in the United States and more than one billion in the world. If this country is to make progress in combating terrorism, it is essential to nurture the confidence of communities like these—and not just the Muslim communities, of course.

"Trust us" is simply not sufficient as reassurance under these circumstances. Unless systems are in place to guarantee transparency and accountability, strong surveillance powers can quickly become self-defeating.

In assessing the Patriot Act and additional surveillance powers that may be proposed, Americans must acknowledge that the threat of terrorism creates a legitimate need for distinctive law enforcement tools. But at the same time, to preserve core freedoms, to reduce the dangers of government abuse, and to achieve genuine security benefits, policymakers also must maintain the traditional commitment to carefully selective approaches, with narrowly tailored powers and maximum feasible accountability.

Chapter 3

TRACKING AL QAEDA
FOREIGN INTELLIGENCE
SEARCHES AND SURVEILLANCE

A powerful tool for fighting international terrorism, the Foreign Intelligence Surveillance Act (FISA) governs searches and electronic surveillance inside the United States that target foreign powers, international terrorist networks, and their agents.[1] FISA quickly became a focus of post–September 11 discussions of "what went wrong," and section 218 of the Patriot Act sought to make FISA even stronger than it already was. Although the Fourth Amendment and related statutes strictly limit most government searches and surveillance, FISA affords broader authority in foreign intelligence matters.

This chapter first reviews the normal constitutional and statutory principles that make FISA's regime of exceptional powers so important. It then assesses the value—and dangers—of the Patriot Act steps to expand FISA. Those steps, though largely justifiable, went much further than necessary and failed to create new safeguards to replace those they had dismantled. Substantial corrective measures are now imperative to keep the FISA process running smoothly and without excesses that will be discovered only when it is too late.

CONSTITUTIONAL AND STATUTORY PRINCIPLES

The legal regime that governs searches and surveillance is a complex mixture of constitutional limits and detailed statutory regulations. Before entering into the details, this section provides a brief overview of the three most important components of that regime: the Fourth Amendment, Title III, and FISA.

THE FOURTH AMENDMENT

The foundation for protecting privacy and limiting government's power to intrude is the Fourth Amendment's prohibition of "unreasonable searches and seizures."[2] Subject to a few narrowly drawn exceptions, the Fourth Amendment permits an investigative search only when it is supported by probable cause and a warrant.[3] That is, investigators must have "a substantial basis" to believe that a search will reveal evidence of criminal activity,[4] and a neutral judicial officer, concurring in that assessment, must authorize the search in a court order that "particularly describ[es] the place to be searched, and the persons or things to be seized."[5]

Several ideas are central to this constitutional regime. One, often misunderstood, is that those who are in fact engaged in criminal activity have no claim to be shielded from governmental intrusion; once probable cause exists, their houses, papers, and effects are fair game for any search that could yield evidence of past or ongoing offenses. The point of the probable cause requirement is not to shield those who "have something to hide" but rather to ensure that searches will focus on individuals who are likely offenders and will not subject innocent, law-abiding citizens to disruptive, frightening, intrusive search and surveillance practices.

The second central idea concerns checks and balances. Hard experience made clear to the Constitution's framers that, without some outside control, investigators in the executive branch, even when acting in good faith, too quickly find "probable cause" and too easily abuse their power to search.[6] The Fourth Amendment therefore requires that the judgment about probable cause ordinarily be made by a neutral judicial officer who will narrowly define the permissible scope of a search before it occurs.[7]

In the atmosphere of intense partisanship that often surrounds discussions of the Patriot Act, it is necessary to stress the obvious point that the requirement of independent judicial approval is not based on doubt about the good intentions of any particular administration. To enforce the warrant requirement, as a unanimous Supreme Court did at the height of the Vietnam War in the so-called *Keith* case,[8] does not reflect any lack of respect for the attorney general currently in power. As most attorneys general have themselves understood, checks and balances—and the warrant requirement in particular—simply reflect the consistent verdict of history that grave abuses are all too likely if investigators—even conscientious, well-trained investigators—are permitted to search without judicial approval. In the *Keith* case the Court acknowledged the "pragmatic force to the Government's position"[9] that a warrant procedure will sometimes make efforts to protect national security more difficult. Nonetheless, the Court held that compliance with the traditional warrant requirement remained essential. Justice Lewis Powell wrote for the Court:[10]

> History abundantly documents the tendency of Government— however benevolent and benign its motives—to view with suspicion those who most fervently dispute its policies. Fourth Amendment protections become the more necessary when the targets of official surveillance may be those suspected of unorthodoxy in their political beliefs.

TITLE III

Because there is a reasonable expectation of privacy in the content of personal communication in most nonpublic settings, these communications can be monitored only on the authority of a warrant supported by probable cause. But the Fourth Amendment prohibits "general" searches (so-called fishing expeditions) and expressly specifies that a valid warrant must "particularly describ[e] the place to be searched, and the persons or things to be seized."[11] A warrant authorizing investigators to record or scan all conversations on a certain phone would violate this particularity requirement, and in 1967 the Supreme Court held unconstitutional a New York statute providing for a judicially issued surveillance warrant that was a "broadside authorization" of this sort.[12]

Congress responded the next year by creating a detailed regime to limit the scope of such surveillance and to enable eavesdropping and wiretapping warrants to meet Fourth Amendment particularity requirements. The statute (commonly known as Title III)[13] permits surveillance only for enumerated, especially serious crimes and requires investigators to convince the court, before it issues a warrant, that the evidence they seek cannot be obtained by using less intrusive investigative tools. The statute limits the time period of surveillance, stipulates a specific showing of need to obtain extensions, and requires efforts to minimize eavesdropping on innocent parties. The statute also mandates prompt reports to the court of the surveillance results and regulates the manner in which the results can be used.[14]

Title III specified, however, that none of its requirements would "limit the constitutional power of the President to take such measures as he deems necessary to protect the United States against [any] clear and present danger to the structure or existence of the Government."[15] This provision seemed to imply that "national security" wiretaps in both domestic and foreign investigations could continue outside the restrictions of Title III, and, since at least 1946 and continuing for several decades, successive attorneys general consistently asserted an inherent presidential power to conduct national security searches and wiretaps without any judicial approval at all.[16] But in 1972 (during the Vietnam War), the *Keith* case held that the president had no such constitutional power with respect to domestic individuals and organizations—those having "no significant connection" with a foreign power.[17] As a result, the Supreme Court ruled, surveillance of domestic targets, even in "clear and present danger" situations, is unconstitutional in the absence of a judicial warrant that meets Fourth Amendment particularity requirements (such as those detailed in Title III).[18] The Court left open the possibility of broader presidential authority to conduct surveillance of foreign powers and their agents, but its expressed misgivings about unchecked executive power made clear that Justice Department probes could be in jeopardy in the absence of carefully tailored statutory safeguards.

FISA

To formalize and regulate the gathering of foreign intelligence, Congress enacted the Foreign Intelligence Surveillance Act in 1978.[19] Like surveillance under Title III, FISA probes can target U.S. citizens as well as foreign governments and foreign nationals. Like Title III, FISA normally prohibits surveillance in the absence of a judicial warrant and imposes time limits and minimization procedures. But FISA provides greatly simplified procedures for obtaining and executing foreign intelligence warrants, and these simplified procedures apply to physical searches as well as electronic surveillance: applications for a FISA warrant go to specially selected federal judges; FISA imposes much less judicial control over the particularity and scope of the surveillance or search; and probable cause to believe that the surveillance or search will reveal evidence of crime is not invariably required. Thus, although FISA requires a court order, the judge's role is far more limited than in domestic law enforcement situations, and the conventional probable cause requirement is much less stringent.

There are several significant prerequisites for FISA surveillance under this distinctive regime. The government must show probable cause (that is, some substantial basis) to believe that the surveillance target, whether an American or foreign national, is the agent of a foreign power, of a foreign-based political organization, or a member of an international terrorist group.[20] If the target is a "United States person" (a citizen or an alien with permanent resident status) FISA requires, in addition, probable cause to believe that the target's activities "may involve" a crime related to clandestine intelligence gathering, terrorism, or identity fraud.[21] And, as FISA stood prior to September 11, the government had to certify that "the purpose of the surveillance is to obtain foreign intelligence information."[22]

Significantly, however, FISA does not require that the person targeted actually must be a foreign spy or an international terrorist. Foreign nationals from friendly countries who do nothing to conceal their activities nonetheless qualify as "foreign agents" subject to broad FISA surveillance simply because they have ties to *legitimate* foreign organizations, and the "foreign intelligence information" that a FISA probe can seek to obtain broadly includes any information that relates to the foreign affairs of the United States. Moreover, even when there is suspicion that the activities of foreign nationals and U.S. citizens "may involve" an intelligence-gathering crime, FISA exposes these individuals to wider, less regulated surveillance that would be unconstitutional if based only on probable cause to believe that the target was a serial killer or rapist.

In sum, FISA allows search and surveillance procedures that are in many respects more flexible than those available in conventional criminal investigations, specifically:

- ◆ FISA authorizes intrusive investigative techniques, such as clandestine physical searches, that are rarely permissible in criminal investigations.

- Surveillance and physical searches can continue over longer periods of time, with less judicial supervision.

- For nonresident foreign nationals, surveillance is permitted after showing only a diluted form of suspicion not equivalent to the traditional criminal standard of probable cause.

- The person targeted, whether a foreigner or a U.S. citizen, normally is *never* notified that he or she was subjected to surveillance or a clandestine search of property or premises.

- If that person is prosecuted, defense attorneys normally cannot review the surveillance documents, as they could if surveillance had been conducted under conventional law enforcement standards.

The premise of FISA is that broader surveillance is justified, with fewer checks, because its aim is not to gather evidence for criminal prosecution but to counter the clandestine intelligence activities of foreign nations and to protect the United States from attack by hostile foreign powers. The courts have uniformly upheld the constitutionality of FISA surveillance under relaxed safeguards because "governmental interests in gathering foreign intelligence are of paramount importance to national security, and may differ substantially from those presented in the normal criminal investigation."[23]

THE FISA PROCESS BEFORE SEPTEMBER 11

Until it burst into public view following September 11, FISA was an obscure statute known only to a few government insiders and to an even smaller number of outside lawyers and academics. The Foreign Intelligence Surveillance Court, meeting secretly in a sealed, secure room in Washington, D.C., received on average about 750 warrant applications per year,[24] and before 2001 it had never rejected an application.[25] Civil liberties groups saw FISA as a large breach in the constitutional and statutory regime of privacy safeguards and understandably viewed the FISA court as little more than a rubber stamp.[26]

The various post–September 11 inquiries opened a window on the FISA process and revealed it to be much more demanding than outsiders had imagined.[27] Justice Department officials in the Office of Intelligence Policy and Review (OIPR), the bureau responsible for vetting FISA applications, pressed hard to make them complete and sufficiently detailed. In addition, they developed rigorous procedures to ensure that prosecutors could not exploit FISA to circumvent the requirements for ordinary criminal warrants. Over time, under pressure from the Foreign Intelligence Surveillance Court and Justice Department attorneys, formal procedures and day-to-day practice became increasingly elaborate. A "wall"—really a complicated series of walls—developed to separate various clusters of law enforcement and intelligence agents. Other major hurdles were not attributable to FISA or legal requirements of any sort: a cumbersome FBI bureaucracy, an antiquated computer system that generated its own bottlenecks, FBI managers who inexplicably obstructed valid FISA applications, and core personnel who misinterpreted the most elementary FISA requirements. The FISA wall was just one challenge in an extraordinarily daunting obstacle course.

MANY PITFALLS, MANY WALLS

Although FISA's requirements contributed to the unhealthy segmentation of law-enforcement and intelligence efforts before September 11, most of the bureaucratic obstacles had nothing to do with FISA, and some of the segmentation attributed to FISA was in fact the product of unrelated agency practices. These dynamics have escaped public attention, but the various inquiries into intelligence shortcomings before September 11 invariably stressed their importance. Putting the FISA wall (that is, the separation of foreign intelligence operations from law enforcement) in context, the joint inquiry of the Senate and House intelligence committees explained:[28]

> The "Wall" is not a single barrier, but a series of restrictions between and within agencies constructed over sixty years as a result of legal, policy, institutional, and personal factors. These walls separate foreign from domestic activities, foreign intelligence from law-enforcement operations, the FBI from the CIA, communications intelligence from other types of intelligence, the Intelligence Community from other federal agencies, and national-security information from other forms of evidence. . . .

Generations of intelligence professionals have been trained in the belief that the CIA should not play any internal security role. They also learned that sensitive information should be disclosed only to those with a demonstrable "need to know." . . . In addition, law enforcement personnel have long recognized that confidentiality, protection of witnesses, and secrecy of grand jury information are essential to the successful investigation and prosecution of crimes. Thus, in the law-enforcement and foreign intelligence professions, security practices and strict limits on sharing information have become second nature.

FBI managers added further roadblocks. As detailed by the Leahy-Grassley-Specter report for the Senate Judiciary Committee,[29] managers at headquarters, on receipt of requests to apply for a FISA warrant, raised unnecessary objections and insisted that agents work to buttress applications that were already more than sufficient. Yet, they themselves failed to give help they were ideally placed to provide, for example, by searching for supplementary information in the broader FBI database. Astonishingly, a Bureau counterterrorism manager holding a key position in the FISA application chain did not know—and admitted he did not know—what FISA's legal requirements were.[30] Yet, this manager blocked valid applications as insufficient or sent them back to the field for more work without bothering to seek guidance from Bureau attorneys.

Even more astonishingly, the Bureau attorneys responsible for giving that guidance misunderstood FISA requirements as well. They incorrectly thought "probable cause" meant "more probable than not" and admitted they were unfamiliar with the leading Supreme Court precedent on the subject, a case that had adopted a much more flexible standard in 1983. Well before September 11, FBI procedural reviews showed clear patterns of insufficient familiarity with FISA, excessive caution, and interposition of supposed legal requirements that did not in fact exist.[31] As the Leahy-Grassley-Specter report concluded, "It is difficult to understand how the agents whose jobs included such a heavy FISA component could not have understood that statute. It is difficult to understand how the FBI could have so failed its own agents in such a crucial aspect of their training."[32]

Similar misunderstandings existed even among OIPR attorneys in the Department of Justice. Their performance came under scrutiny well before September 11, as a result of missteps in the Wen Ho Lee case, a 1990s investigation into suspected leaking of classified information about nuclear weapons at Los Alamos National Laboratory. An audit of that investigation, completed in May 2000, established that OIPR had blocked valid FISA applications by insisting on an overly stringent standard of probable cause and concluded that OIPR's near-perfect track record before the FISA Court was paradoxically "proof of error, rather than proof of excellence."[33] In combination, these Justice Department and FBI failures posed an often insuperable obstacle to the effective use of FISA, and they would have done so regardless of how FISA's legal mandates had been formulated.

The Bureau's handling of the Zacarias Moussaoui search request, described more fully in Chapter 2, makes clear that these failures cannot be attributed to the FISA "wall" between intelligence gathering and law enforcement.[34] When the Minneapolis field office asked headquarters to seek a FISA warrant to search Moussaoui's computer, a supervisor at headquarters incorrectly informed agent Coleen Rowley that more information was required to establish that Moussaoui was a foreign agent within the meaning of FISA. No legal barrier, only his own capacities, prevented this supervisor from helping her fill any information gap by drawing on important additional details that were available in his own database. And when French intelligence established Moussaoui's ties to an international terrorist group, this supervisor, believing that such groups did not qualify as foreign powers, denied the request again.[35]

The supervisor's understanding of the "foreign power" requirement was simply incorrect, and inexplicably so. For a foreign national like Moussaoui, FISA required probable cause to believe that the target of the search was involved with any group of individuals who commit or plan acts of international terrorism.[36] That standard, which the Patriot Act left intact, was not difficult to meet in Moussaoui's case.[37] Once again, time pressure, resource constraints, grossly deficient training, and a culture of extreme caution prevented effective use of strong powers that were readily available.

THE FISA WALL

FISA's criteria nonetheless spawned further complexity. Before September 11 the FISA regime was available only when "*the* purpose of the surveillance [or physical search] is to obtain foreign intelligence information."[38] In addition, the statute required (and still requires) "minimization" procedures to limit the retention and dissemination of information relating to U.S. persons.[39] As a result, beginning in the

1980s, the Department of Justice took the view that FISA was unavailable when the government's primary purpose was not merely to gather intelligence but to amass evidence for criminal prosecution.[40] The statute explicitly contemplated that if a FISA surveillance uncovered evidence of crime, the evidence could be transmitted to prosecutors and would be admissible at the criminal trial.[41] But Justice officials nonetheless insisted that the permissive FISA regime be used only when foreign intelligence objectives were paramount.[42] And to guard against any appearance that this requirement was being flouted, the FBI and Justice Department adopted procedures, originally informal ones, to guarantee a strictly "one-way" flow of information: intelligence agents could pass FISA information to prosecutors, but prosecutors could not seek to direct or influence the FISA investigators.[43]

Over time, Justice officials grew increasingly concerned that evidence of consultation between prosecutors and intelligence agents could jeopardize subsequent efforts to charge foreign agents with intelligence crimes. The 1994 espionage prosecution of Aldrich Ames brought these concerns to the fore and prompted OIPR to insist on a system of formal approvals with rigorous control, to limit contacts across the divide between foreign intelligence operations and prosecution, and to regulate the sharing of information.[44] In 1995 the attorney general issued procedures to that effect; the Foreign Intelligence Surveillance Court was duly informed and then treated these "minimization" safeguards as an integral part of its own regime for issuing warrants.[45] It became customary for warrant applications to detail all consultations between FISA agents and prosecution teams whenever overlapping intelligence and criminal investigations were under way. Minor modifications were made in January 2000, and the revised minimization procedures were carried forward in the new administration. In August 2001 the deputy attorney general reaffirmed the procedures and added further requirements to them.[46]

These minimization procedures, far more elaborate than the statute itself required, were adopted as prophylactic measures to forestall any possible challenge to compliance with the "purpose" requirement that FISA surveillance be confined to obtaining foreign intelligence. Nonetheless, in an environment in which segmentation was already the order of the day, the procedures produced stresses in two opposing directions. First, whether because of misunderstanding or bureaucratic habit, agents assumed that consultation and information sharing were restricted even more than the already overbroad procedures actually called for. FBI agents thought they could not share FISA information with agents on other teams, and many even thought they could not share non-FISA information.[47]

Second, when minimization procedures were not met in FISA surveillance cases, relations between the FBI and the Foreign Intelligence Surveillance Court grew strained. In September 2000 the Justice Department informed the court that seventy-five previous FISA applications had misstated contacts across the intelligence/prosecution divide.[48] A series of tense interchanges between the Justice Department and the court resulted. In April 2001, in an effort to guarantee careful vetting of applications, the FBI promulgated yet more elaborate procedures, but not before the court had barred one FBI agent from appearing before it at all.[49] That step prompted a further round of excessive caution. Agents on the FISA side "feared the fate of the agent who had been barred and began to avoid even the most pedestrian contact with personnel in criminal components of the Bureau or DOJ."[50] Prosecutors attempting to "connect the dots" were free to talk to anyone in the world—except the government agents who could be most helpful, their counterparts on FBI task forces across the street.[51] And, as tensions with the Foreign Intelligence Surveillance Court boiled over in the spring and summer of 2001, a large number of FISA surveillances (including many related to international terrorism) were allowed to lapse.[52] In other instances, however, FISA warrants expired simply because managers at headquarters failed to complete routine paperwork.[53]

The "purpose" requirement was thus a seed from which increasingly intricate obstacles developed. Yet, the resulting problems were not inevitable, even under the law as it stood before September 11; most of the difficulties probably could have been avoided with better training, more common sense, and more willingness to tolerate ambiguity and decentralized discretion.

FISA DEVELOPMENTS AFTER SEPTEMBER 11

DISMANTLING THE WALL

The Patriot Act attacked the "wall" in two ways. First, section 504 specifically authorized agents who conduct FISA searches and surveillance to coordinate with law enforcement officials, and it provided that such coordination would not preclude FISA agents from certifying that their investigation had the required foreign intelligence purpose.[54] Second, to guard further against any risk that courts might object to the mingling of law-enforcement and foreign-intelligence functions, section 218 changed the way the nettlesome "purpose" clause was formulated. It eliminated the requirement that gathering foreign intelligence must be "the" purpose of the surveillance and instead made it sufficient that "a *significant* purpose of the surveillance [or physical search] is to obtain foreign intelligence information."[55]

In rewriting the "purpose" clause, Congress did not intend to dilute the legal requirements for obtaining a FISA warrant.[56] Rather, the reason for relaxing the "purpose" formula was simply to tear down the "wall." The new language would restore flexibility in two ways: a decision to initiate FISA surveillance would no longer be perceived as endangering subsequent prosecution of the target, and the agents involved would no longer be precluded from consulting officials on the law enforcement side. Although section 218 sunsets automatically in December 2005,[57] the coordination provisions of section 504, which accomplish largely the same results as section 218, do not.

RELAXING FISA'S RESTRICTIONS

The Patriot Act made FISA more flexible in four other respects. It provided more scope for using pen registers and "roving" surveillance, enlarged the opportunities for clandestine physical searches, and extended the time periods for FISA investigations.*

PEN REGISTERS UNDER FISA. Section 214 of the Patriot Act clarified the procedures for installing "pen-register" and "trap/trace" devices in FISA investigations. (These terms originally referred to devices designed to record telephone numbers dialed. Chapter 5 discusses their implications for privacy.) Section 214 does not in itself enlarge

---

*One of the Patriot Act amendments to FISA does not warrant extended discussion. Section 225 makes clear that private individuals and firms cannot be sued for actions taken to comply with law-enforcement orders issued under FISA. Although this provision sunsets in December 2005, it should not be considered controversial.

the government's surveillance powers. If anything, its language slightly restricts the requirements that prior FISA law had set for pen-register and trap/trace surveillance of U.S. citizens. Although section 214, which sunsets in December 2005, should not be controversial, it has important implications, because the Patriot Act elsewhere extends significantly the definition of "pen-register" and "trap/trace" devices, and that extended definition (which does not sunset) automatically carries over from the domestic surveillance statutes to FISA. As a result, the concerns about broad pen-register authority likewise carry over to FISA. Section 214 should not be renewed without amendments (parallel to those discussed in Chapter 5) to rein it in.

ROVING SURVEILLANCE. Patriot Act section 206 addresses the problem of "roving" surveillance. Prior to September 11, statutes allowed investigators in certain domestic law enforcement situations to obtain warrants for a "roving" surveillance that targets a suspect wherever that person may be rather than homing in on a particular telephone or e-mail account. But such warrants are exceptional, and the statute permits them only when a court finds that the suspect has taken evasive action that could thwart ordinary surveillance measures.[58] Section 206 authorizes roving surveillance in FISA investigations as well.

Roving surveillance has been challenged as a violation of the explicit Fourth Amendment requirement that a warrant must "particularly describ[e] the place to be searched."[59] But the argument is much less plausible than this straightforward language would suggest. As written, the Fourth Amendment protects only "persons, houses, papers and effects." Because words are not tangible things of that sort, the Fourth Amendment, if applied literally, would not protect against wiretapping and electronic surveillance at all.[60]

In expanding the reach of the Fourth Amendment to safeguard reasonable expectations of privacy in a more general sense,[61] the Supreme Court adapted the Constitution to the dangers to privacy posed by modern technology. It would be paradoxical to reinterpret the Fourth Amendment in this functional way, to prohibit warrantless electronic surveillance, but then to insist that the only acceptable warrants must be ones that authorize the surveillance of tangible places and things. It seems more reasonable to require only that a warrant satisfy the functional objectives of the particularity requirement, for example, by describing the person to be targeted and the reasons why the location itself cannot be specified. On this basis, courts have uniformly upheld the constitutionality of roving surveillance.

Though the constitutional issue has been settled, only the domestic law enforcement statutes authorized roving surveillance explicitly. As a result, that tactic was available in narcotics, fraud, and racketeering probes but not in foreign intelligence investigations, an area where the government normally has more latitude. Section 206 corrects that anomaly by authorizing roving surveillance in FISA investigations, subject to the same conditions that apply to such surveillance in conventional law enforcement. Although section 206 sunsets automatically in December 2005, the roving surveillance authority, long accepted in the domestic law enforcement sphere, should not be considered controversial.

TIME PERIODS. Section 207 increased the time periods allowed for electronic surveillance and physical searches of an agent who is a "non-U.S. person" (someone not a U.S. citizen or resident). For citizens, section 207 did not change the time limits applicable to electronic surveillance, but it doubled, from forty-five to ninety days, the period during which citizens can be subjected to clandestine physical searches.[62]

This sort of fine tuning is emblematic of the Patriot Act and a perfect illustration of why its supporters and critics see it in such contradictory terms. The act did not sweep away the time limits completely. Yet, it subjected nonresident foreign nationals to long periods of largely unregulated monitoring that would be far out of bounds if these individuals were the targets of an ordinary criminal investigation. (The normal time limit for a law enforcement surveillance under Title III is thirty days, and extensions are strictly limited.[63]) And, much worse, section 207 makes a genuinely alarming change in the limits applicable to clandestine physical searches of U.S. citizens and nonresidents alike.

CLANDESTINE PHYSICAL SEARCHES. In law enforcement matters, clandestine searches—to be discussed in depth in Chapter 5—are subject to especially tight controls: the need for secrecy must be compelling; the search must be made in a narrow window of time; and the target of the search normally must be notified shortly thereafter, usually within seven days.[64] In contrast, a clandestine FISA search is more easily authorized, can be conducted over considerable time (now extending to renewable three-month periods), and is not merely a "delayed notification" search; the targets of a clandestine FISA search are never notified that their homes were secretly inspected or that their documents and other property were surreptitiously copied or seized.[65] Section 207 sunsets automatically in December 2005; an especially close look seems warranted for its provision allowing FBI agents to conduct clandestine searches against U.S. citizens over an extended period without showing any special need for secrecy.

USING THE NEW FISA

To no one's surprise, government use of FISA warrants has exploded since passage of the Patriot Act. The 1,724 FISA warrants approved in calendar year 2003 represent an 85 percent increase over the comparable figure for 2001.[66] But the Foreign Intelligence Surveillance Court apparently continues to give warrant applications close scrutiny. In 2003 the court denied four applications and made substantive modifications in seventy-nine others.[67]

For critics of section 218, the mushrooming of FISA applications might be seen as confirmation of fears that prosecutors would exploit FISA to circumvent the tighter limits and more stringent oversight that criminal warrants entail. But it seems likely that the lion's share of the increase (and possibly all of it) results from the increase in terror-related intelligence investigations rather than from a migration of criminal cases into the FISA process. In fact, federal applications for ordinary criminal surveillance warrants also have increased steadily since 2001.[68]

While expanding its use of FISA, the Justice Department took steps after September 11 to relax the procedures that had impeded communication between law enforcement and intelligence agents. Until that time departmental regulations had barred prosecutors from intentionally or inadvertently "directing or controlling the [foreign intelligence] investigation toward law enforcement objectives."[69] The principal concern, of course, was to prevent prosecutors lacking grounds for a conventional warrant from instructing FISA teams to conduct expanded surveillance as part of a fishing expedition seeking to build an ordinary criminal case.

Other concerns about prosecutors misusing FISA are less dramatic but in practical terms equally important. When a U.S. citizen is
the target, the threshold requirements for obtaining a FISA warrant
are usually no easier to meet than those for obtaining a Title III criminal warrant. The difference, however, is that a FISA warrant can
remain in effect for longer periods of time, with less oversight, less difficulty in getting renewals, and only optional review by the issuing
court when the surveillance is completed. In all these respects, the
Title III regime guarantees much tighter supervision.[70]

The Title III regime also promotes better accountability through
a stronger system of sanctions. Compared to Title III, FISA affords relatively weak remedies for surveillance targets who are eventually
prosecuted for crime, and it affords distinct but even weaker remedies
for surveillance targets who are not prosecuted.[71] In the case of individuals targeted for clandestine physical searches, FISA's remedies are
especially slight relative to those available following clandestine
searches under a law enforcement warrant.[72] In all these respects, the
FISA regime offers less accountability and thus an enhanced risk of
overly invasive surveillance and other abuses. There is a correspond-
ingly strong need to ensure that prosecutors do not exploit the FISA
regime to circumvent the safeguards available when searches and surveillance are conducted under normal law enforcement procedures.

Nonetheless, when Attorney General John Ashcroft revised the
FISA minimization regulations in March 2002, he instructed FBI and
Justice Department officials that, because of the Patriot Act's relaxation
of the "purpose" requirement, FISA powers could now "be used primarily for a law enforcement purpose, so long as a significant foreign
intelligence purpose remains."[73] To this end, he authorized prosecutors
pursuing criminal cases to give advice to foreign intelligence investigators concerning the "initiation . . . or expansion of FISA searches or
surveillance," and he deleted the caveat that had barred prosecutors
from "directing or controlling" the scope of FISA surveillance.[74]

To support this approach, which opens the door to a large prosecutorial role in the loosely regulated FISA procedures, the
Department of Justice made two distinct points. First, the department argued that because the statutory language no longer requires
a primary purpose related to intelligence gathering, it necessarily
implies that the primary purpose can be something else. As a result,
the department claimed that the statute now allows the use of FISA
surveillance even when the investigator's primary goal is to build

evidence to prosecute the target of an ordinary crime (tax evasion, for example), so long as the department can still certify in good faith that a significant subsidiary purpose of the probe is to protect the United States by gathering foreign intelligence.

Second, and even more broadly, the department argued that, apart from any purely preventive intelligence function, criminal prosecution is itself an effective means to protect the United States from foreign attack by putting spies and terrorists out of business. As a result, the department insisted that when the target is believed to be a "foreign agent," as FISA requires, the statute's "significant purpose" requirement would be met even when the government's *sole* objective was to prosecute the target for an ordinary federal crime.

In May 2002 the Foreign Intelligence Surveillance Court unanimously rejected the Justice Department's approach. Relying on the FISA provision that requires procedures to minimize the acquisition of information not necessary for foreign intelligence purposes, the court ruled that "law enforcement officials *shall not* make recommendations to intelligence officials concerning the initiation . . . or expansion of FISA searches or surveillance."[75] The court insisted, moreover, that Justice Department regulations must make certain that prosecutors "*do not* direct or control the use of the FISA procedures to enhance criminal prosecution."[76] The court noted tartly that any need for prosecutors to guide "the use of highly intrusive FISA surveillances . . . is yet to be explained."[77]

The Justice Department, however, appealed that ruling to another obscure body, the Foreign Intelligence Surveillance Court of Review.* That court likewise rejected the department's most sweeping arguments for allowing prosecutors to use FISA as a tool of criminal investigation. The court declared that Congress presupposed a dichotomy between prosecution and purely preventive intelligence gathering. As a result, FISA cannot, as the Justice Department had argued, be used when the government's sole objective is criminal prosecution, even prosecution intended to disable a foreign agent.[78] In addition, when intelligence gathering is a genuine subsidiary purpose

---

*The Foreign Intelligence Surveillance Court of Review had never before met, and it heard arguments only from the Justice Department, technically the only party to the case. The court did, however, accept amicus curiae briefs supporting the FISA court's decision from the ACLU and other groups.

of the surveillance and criminal prosecution its primary purpose, the criminal case nonetheless must involve foreign intelligence offenses; denying another of the Justice Department's broad claims, the court declared that "the FISA process cannot be used as a device to investigate wholly unrelated ordinary crimes."[79]

Having rejected the most troubling and least restrictive interpretations of the Patriot Act's "significant purpose" requirement, the review court nonetheless reversed the ruling of the FISA trial judges and upheld the contested provisions of the Ashcroft memorandum.[80] It concluded that Congress did indeed authorize prosecutors to use FISA in criminal investigations (and therefore to "direct or control" it), provided only that their goal is to charge a foreign intelligence crime and that a genuine primary or subsidiary purpose of the surveillance is preventive intelligence gathering. The court ruled, moreover, that, given the importance of the counterterrorism effort, these exceptional powers are not unconstitutional. For now, the conclusions of the court of review are final because the only party to the case, the Justice Department, prevailed. The Supreme Court will have an opportunity to speak to the issue only when evidence acquired through expanded FISA surveillance is introduced against a defendant in a criminal prosecution. Even if the Court agrees that broad prosecutorial access to FISA is not unconstitutional, those involved in shaping law enforcement policy must assess whether the approach reflected in the 2002 Ashcroft memorandum is unwise.

NAVIGATING THE FISA DILEMMA

Controversy persists about whether effective surveillance of terrorist suspects necessitates breaking down the "wall" that traditionally has blocked law enforcement agents' access to broad FISA powers. September 11 made clear that a rigid division between law-enforcement and foreign-intelligence operations can be artificial and counterproductive in the context of fighting international terrorist groups like al Qaeda. When threats emanate from terrorist groups that combine the elusive features of a criminal conspiracy with the most dangerous powers (and none of the restraining responsibilities) of a foreign state, there is often little practical difference between criminal and foreign intelligence investigations. The Foreign Intelligence Surveillance Court of Review rightly stressed this point but then, in a non sequitur, concluded that prosecutors could safely be allowed to assume the lead role. Yet law enforcement can easily slide into prosecutorial fishing expeditions and other dangers to a free society when it operates free of close judicial scrutiny.

The importance of containing both dangers—that of international terrorism and the less obvious but significant hazard of prosecutorial abuse—suggests the court of review's all-or-nothing approach is unwarranted. Flexibility to give prosecutors any evidence of crime obtained in foreign intelligence operations was always part of the FISA system and can be enhanced without significant danger to basic Fourth Amendment values. The risk of overreaching arises when broad FISA tools are used to pursue purely law enforcement goals. In a world of boundless resources, therefore, it would surely make sense to insist that law enforcement and counterterrorism investigators be confined to distinct teams.

The flaw in that reasoning, as the Court of Review emphasized, is that resources are limited. But the court accepted much too readily the budgetary baseline that happens to be set now. A serious commitment to the preservation of liberty requires allocating sufficient funds to make reasonable accountability measures a reality.

The problem of limited human resources is not so easily solved. At the highest levels of the FBI and the Justice Department, senior executives will almost inevitably have responsibility for both functions. And barriers to a blending of roles could (rightly or out of excess caution) inhibit efforts to use criminal investigators in the field for vital counterterrorism measures.

What seems hard to justify, even against this background, is the core of the Ashcroft innovation, the provision granting the department's litigating prosecutors the power to *initiate* FISA surveillance and to enlarge its scope, in order to develop evidence for a criminal case. Here, as the decision of FISA's lower court judges had stressed, flexibility and appropriate coordination are no longer at issue. Rather, the Ashcroft remedy makes FISA's highly intrusive, lightly supervised surveillance powers available for objectives not primarily concerned with preventive intelligence gathering. The need for some blending of functions does not come close to justifying a regime in which prosecutors can avoid normal systems of oversight by initiating and directing the use of FISA. As the lower court's initial decision recognized, the need for prosecutors to control the scope of preventive surveillance has never been explained.

SOLUTIONS TO THE FOREIGN INTELLIGENCE PUZZLE

Three points emerge from the preceding discussion. First, some blending of intelligence-gathering and law-enforcement functions is inevitable in pursuing an effective counterterrorism strategy. Second, even in areas where the two functions in principle can be kept distinct, the day-to-day realities of attempting to do so will generate a cumbersome process laden with pitfalls that far outweigh the benefits that flow from maintaining a clean separation. Third, however, granting prosecutors carte blanche to invoke FISA, rather than ordinary criminal law processes, poses significant risks in four areas: overly intrusive surveillance, dangerously diluted oversight, weakened remedies, and impairment of the tools of effective defense for individuals ultimately charged with crimes. In short, we should dismantle the wall, but we must find other, less cumbersome safeguards to replace it. We must not and need not sacrifice all the protections that the wall, in its awkward fashion, had sought to achieve.

Many members of Congress are already attentive to this concern. Several proposals for amending FISA were introduced in the 2004 session, and most will likely be on the legislative agenda again in 2005.

One, the so-called lone-wolf amendment, was enacted in December 2004 as part of the Intelligence Reform Act.[81] It permits the use of FISA not only when the target is involved with a foreign-based group but also when the suspect is believed to be acting alone, provided that he or she is a foreign citizen who "engages in international terrorism or activities in preparation therefore."[82]

The lone-wolf amendment seeks to counter a weakness in FISA that purportedly excuses the FBI failure to search Zacarias Moussaoui's effects after his arrest in August 2001. But, as the post–September 11 inquiries have documented, the information available at that juncture was amply sufficient to obtain a warrant under FISA as it stood.[83] If (contrary to the evidence) there had been a problem in that instance, the new provision would not necessarily solve it: any perceived gaps in the information available at that time also would have made it difficult to show that Moussaoui was a "lone wolf" because the amended FISA provision still requires probable cause to believe that a person like Moussaoui was "engage[d] in international terrorism or activities in preparation therefore." As the bipartisan Leahy-Grassley-Specter report concluded, the lone-wolf proposal, whatever its intent, has had the effect of diverting attention from an inexcusable FBI failure and from necessary but more difficult reform in such areas as training, supervision, coordination, and computer capabilities.[84] The lone-wolf provision sunsets in December 2005. It should not be renewed unless the Justice Department can clearly explain the need for it and can show that it is making sufficient progress in correcting its far more important institutional deficiencies.

The remainder of the proposals offer steps in the other direction, primarily by seeking more disclosure of statistics about FISA activity to the public or congressional oversight committees.[85] One proposal seeks to remove some of the obstacles facing a criminal defendant at trial if he attempts to challenge the legality of a previous FISA surveillance.[86] To date, none of the proposals seeks to tighten the "significant purpose" requirement or to limit in any more direct way the risks of prosecutorial abuse.

A balanced approach to FISA reform should acknowledge the statute's value, the awkwardness of trying to overregulate its use, and at the same time the importance of restoring adequate safeguards. Two areas call for remedial action: enhancing oversight and restraining FISA's reach.

ENHANCING OVERSIGHT

Given the breadth of FISA powers, it is especially important to ensure that effective oversight mechanisms are in place. As the Leahy-Grassley-Specter report stresses, current circumstances do not obviate the need for oversight; they increase it dramatically.[87] Yet, the Department of Justice, rather than acknowledge and cooperate in that process, has often resisted it.[88]

The most effective form of oversight may be individual scrutiny, case by case, by the judge who issues the FISA warrant. The Foreign Intelligence Surveillance Court does conscientiously fulfill its statutory mandate to examine the basis for a FISA application and the minimization procedures proposed. But the judge's obligations after that point are minimal. The statute provides that during the course of the surveillance or when it ends, he or she "may" assess compliance with the minimization procedures.[89] FISA, unlike Title III, does not *require* investigators to report back to the court on the surveillance and minimization results. That loophole should be closed.

Public and congressional oversight also is essential, but that cannot occur if the Department of Justice provides no information about the FISA process. Until recently, Foreign Intelligence Surveillance Court opinions and Justice Department guidance documents were kept secret even when complete documents or a redacted version of them could have been disclosed without difficulty, and the only public report required was an annual statement of the total number of FISA applications filed and approved.[90] In contrast to the information published for Title III criminal warrants (a forty-page statistical report that includes thirteen detailed tables),[91] the FISA report was a letter of less than a page and a half, and it gave no breakdown indicating even such elementary information as the distribution of warrants between electronic and physical searches or between targets who were and were not U.S. citizens.

The Intelligence Reform Act of 2004 takes a modest step in the direction of more useful disclosure.[92] It requires the Justice Department to report to Congress semiannually the number of individuals targeted under FISA for electronic surveillance, physical searches, and pen-registers, and the number of individuals monitored under the new "lone-wolf" surveillance authority. It also requires disclosure of Foreign Intelligence Surveillance Court opinions that include significant interpretations of the statute, consequential legal interpretations presented to the court by the Department of Justice, and the number of times in each reporting period that information obtained through FISA surveillance has been approved for use in a criminal prosecution.

Even so, reporting under FISA remains unjustifiably sketchy. There is still no required disclosure of the number of U.S. citizens who are subjected to each type of FISA surveillance. And, unlike the detailed statistics reported for Title III monitoring, the FISA reports give no indication, even in aggregate statistics, of the kinds of locations where surveillance occurred, the average length of initial surveillance and extensions, or the number of targets subsequently arrested and convicted. Such vital information is the starting point for adequate public understanding of—and confidence in—the FISA process.

Another dimension of effective oversight is a system of meaningful remedies so that agents responsible for abusing the FISA process can be held accountable. Section 223 of the Patriot Act created a civil damage remedy for persons illegally targeted by a FISA investigation. But the civil action is virtually meaningless because those individuals, unless subsequently prosecuted, can virtually never learn that they had been under surveillance.[93] Congress must explore ways to make section 223 more than a dead letter. After-the-fact review, either by the Foreign Intelligence Surveillance Court or by an official in the Justice Department's Office of the Inspector General, could provide one means to identify questionable FISA practices, and in such cases FISA targets could be notified so that they could seek a neutral determination of their rights. Other ways are available to enable more frequent notification of targets, for example in the physical search situations to be discussed below.

Finally, in the case of individuals subsequently charged with crimes, FISA permits a motion to suppress evidence obtained by illegal surveillance.[94] But FISA tightly restricts defense access to relevant information and requires the judge, if the attorney general so requests, to hold the hearing "ex parte"—that is, without hearing argument from the defense side at all.[95] At a minimum, the judge must be allowed to hold an adversary hearing when circumstances do not make secrecy imperative.[96] When sensitive information is involved, the Classified Information Procedures Act provides a balanced mechanism for affording defense counsel the access necessary for a fair trial.[97]

RESTRAINING FISA's REACH

The low threshold prerequisites for invoking FISA are probably the most troubling area but also the most difficult to adjust without interfering with legitimate investigative needs. The standard for electronic surveillance of a U.S. person requires probable cause to suspect commission (or, in limited instances, the possible commission) of a foreign intelligence crime. That approach, present since FISA's inception, relaxes traditional Fourth Amendment requirements only in narrow, reasonably justifiable ways,[98] and there is no need to tighten it.

For nonresident foreign nationals, FISA permits electronic surveillance without probable cause to believe a crime is being committed.[99] It is enough, for example, that the individual is an employee of a foreign-based political organization and that the surveillance is seeking information that relates in any way to "the foreign affairs of the United States."[100] A foreign national working for Greenpeace could easily qualify. This broad power is perhaps understandable when preventive intelligence gathering is the sole purpose, but it becomes especially troubling when a prosecutor initiates a FISA surveillance, as the Ashcroft memorandum permits, with the primary purpose of gathering evidence for a criminal proceeding. In upholding that power of initiation, the court of review dealt only with the surveillance of U.S. citizens and stressed that such probes must involve suspicions related to foreign intelligence crimes.[101] It accordingly did not consider the constitutionality of FISA surveillance directed by prosecutors in other situations. Absent some persuasive explanation of the need for prosecutorial involvement in such cases, it would seem wise to bar law enforcement officials from initiating or controlling FISA surveillance in cases not involving objective suspicions of criminal conduct.

Clandestine physical searches are an especially troubling area because agents using FISA need not show any special need for secrecy and because notification of the search is not merely delayed—normally in a FISA search the homeowner is never notified at all.[102] In both respects FISA permits secrecy that the Fourth Amendment clearly prohibits outside the intelligence-gathering context. Yet, there has been no public outcry over FISA's expanded potential for clandestine physical searches, a surprising omission in light of the tempest surrounding use of the much milder "delayed notification" search power in ordinary law enforcement.

To be sure, the Patriot Act did not relax the already loose criteria for these secret FISA searches. But the "significant purpose" language makes those searches much more readily available, and the Ashcroft memorandum now permits prosecutors to initiate and control their use. When such a search targets a U.S. person, it must be supported by probable cause to suspect a foreign intelligence crime.[103] But even so, the lack of notification raises substantial constitutional concerns because the Fourth Amendment requires prompt notification even when there is probable cause to suspect the most serious criminal misconduct. The court of review decision, focused on an application for electronic surveillance, does not mention the special problems posed by physical searches, and the opinion therefore leaves open the possible unconstitutionality of the Ashcroft procedures in this context.

Congressional action to restrain these secret physical searches clearly seems warranted. No doubt, foreign intelligence matters often involve legitimate needs to withhold (or at least delay) notification. But that is no justification for allowing such searches without any showing of necessity at all. Notification at some point—if not at the outset then later—is a vital component in any regime of effective protection against governmental overreaching. Congress should amend FISA's physical search provisions to permit secrecy only when the necessity for it is demonstrated. Similarly, when the initial entry is clandestine, Congress should require that subsequent notice be given within a specified period (for example, thirty days), absent a further showing of necessity.

In all these respects, the Patriot Act amendments to FISA, legitimate as many of them are, went much further than they should have. Moreover, the act failed to create adequate safeguards commensurate with the broad new authorities it granted. Rather than simply renewing section 218 as it stands, Congress must ensure that the new, more flexible FISA does not open the door to the abuses that the "wall" once served to prevent.

Chapter 4

ACCESSING DOCUMENTS AND RECORDS

In addition to granting foreign intelligence investigators new search and surveillance powers, the Patriot Act allows them much easier access to previously confidential business, financial, and personal records. It expands two little-known but important record-gathering tools: document production orders issued by the Foreign Intelligence Surveillance Court and national security letters issued directly by the FBI. These tools provide a path around the regime governing conventional subpoenas and override the safeguards that subpoena procedures normally afford to important documents and records.

THE PRE–SEPTEMBER 11 SAFEGUARDS

SEARCHES VERSUS SUBPOENAS
(DOCUMENT PRODUCTION ORDERS AND THE LIKE)

Searches, needless to say, are intrusive and often frightening exercises of government power. A police officer or FBI agent appears at the door, enters forcibly if necessary, and physically takes away the homeowner's property. But when there is no need to take the person holding the items by surprise, the law provides less intrusive ways to obtain the same information. For example, a grand jury subpoena can require an individual to deliver records, documents, or other items to government investigators. Less well known than the grand jury subpoena are certain more specialized mechanisms—administrative subpoenas, Foreign Intelligence Surveillance Court orders, and national security letters. These devices, despite important differences, are all similar in directing an individual to produce a specific kind of information.

A subpoena ordering the recipient to turn over information obviously impinges on privacy, and Fourth Amendment principles therefore come into play.[1] But because a subpoena is so much less intrusive than an unannounced, forcible search, courts do not impose the safeguards that a search would require, that is, probable cause and a warrant particularly describing the things to be seized. Instead, the recipient of a subpoena gets an important procedural option not available to the target of a search: he or she can challenge the subpoena prior to releasing the information. The subpoena recipient can ask a court to quash the subpoena and normally will then get a hearing for the judge to consider and rule on objections before ordering compliance.

In practice, the requirements for a valid subpoena are minimal. Normally a challenge succeeds only when the recipient can show that the information sought is protected by some privilege or is not relevant to a legitimate inquiry. Nonetheless, judicial oversight, even in this highly diluted form, does act as a check on unrestricted official snooping, and it provides the subpoena recipient an important guarantee of accountability.

The catch, however, is that in many recurring situations, the privacy interests at stake are not primarily those of the subpoena recipient. Consider, for example, a subpoena directing a bank to produce the checking account records of a particular customer. The bank could move to quash the subpoena, but it may have little motivation to do so. The bank's own privacy interests are not directly affected, only those of its customer. Yet, the customer would not normally have any chance to object to the subpoena and might not even be aware of it. In this common, two-party situation, therefore, a subpoena does not afford the person most affected the necessary opportunity to participate in compliance and ensure accountability. Instead—from the perspective of the bank's customer—a subpoena to the bank is in effect a clandestine search. It would be reasonable to argue that before investigators compel a bank to turn over a customer's records, they should be required to obtain a search warrant supported by probable cause.

The Fourth Amendment requires precisely this approach in many two-party situations. For example, if police want to search a hotel room, they cannot simply ask the hotel management to let them in. Absent consent from the hotel guest, police must have a search warrant.[2] The same rule applies if police want a landlord to give them access to a tenant's apartment.[3]

In the case of documents and records, however, a second important catch comes into play. In a series of controversial decisions in the 1970s, the Supreme Court ruled that the Fourth Amendment offers the citizen *no protection at all* for the privacy of information entrusted to others, such as financial records held by a person's bank or phone records held by a telecommunications company.[4] Under the same principle, the Fourth Amendment does not protect many other documents that most Americans consider highly personal and confidential, such as medical records, personnel records kept by employers, or a student's educational records. The Court reasoned that an individual could not have a reasonable expectation of privacy for this sort of information because he or she had "voluntarily" exposed it to others and necessarily took the risk that people with access to it would turn it over to the government.

Many privacy advocates and ordinary citizens find this reasoning strained. In modern life, the decision to expose one's financial transactions to a bank is not in any meaningful sense a "voluntary" choice. Indeed, the Court's approach paradoxically allows self-protection by actual criminals (who of course can choose to conduct their illegal transactions in cash) while leaving the law-abiding citizen with no practical way to shield the privacy of daily life. It is even less plausible to think that an individual who is ill "voluntarily" exposes his or her private health records to the hospital that is providing treatment. The organizations holding such records typically promise to keep them confidential, just as a hotel in effect promises that it will not rummage through personal effects that a guest leaves in the room. Even if a customer inevitably takes a risk that some companies and their employees might break such promises, the Supreme Court gave prosecutors something much broader—the power to compel the firm to turn over customer information in instances when it would otherwise seek to honor its commitment to preserve confidentiality. This approach deprives the person most affected of *both* the customary forms of accountability, the probable cause warrant required for a search and the prior judicial review that person could seek if he or she had received a subpoena directly.

Congress recognized that this approach left inadequate safeguards for confidential personal information; it responded to the Court's narrow constitutional decisions by imposing statutory limits on government access to financial records, student records held by schools and colleges, and several other categories of sensitive information.[5] Confidentiality provisions of state law add another layer of protection. These statutes do not provide the full complement of Fourth Amendment safeguards, nor do they establish any one system of norms. Instead, they weave a dense web of accountability provisions, with requirements and procedures that differ according to the kind of information concerned and the government's asserted purpose in seeking it.

The Right to Financial Privacy Act (RFPA) is illustrative. Under RFPA, government agents must obtain a grand jury subpoena when they seek access to financial information for an ordinary criminal investigation. Before complying with the subpoena, the bank must give notice to its customer, and customers who object have the right to a hearing at which a court must decide whether the records are relevant to a legitimate governmental inquiry.[6] Similarly, under the Family Educational Rights and Privacy Act (FERPA), an educational institution faced with a subpoena must notify the student whose records are implicated (or the parents, in the cases of a minor) and must give the affected family the opportunity to file a court challenge before it turns over the records.[7]

FISA COURT ORDERS AND NATIONAL SECURITY LETTERS

Even before September 11, the government was allowed more leeway in foreign intelligence investigations. The Foreign Intelligence Surveillance Act (FISA) authorizes the Foreign Intelligence Surveillance Court to issue an unusual type of subpoena. Like any other subpoena, this document production order directs the recipient to turn over designated records of a client or customer, but—unlike a subpoena—the court order does not allow the client or customer to contest the demand. In fact, the order prohibits the recipient from ever revealing to anyone that the records had been sought by the government.[8]

Without such notice and without any opportunity for the individual concerned to challenge the court order, safeguards against abuse are extremely weak. Nonetheless, the required participation of a Foreign Intelligence Surveillance Court judge provides some minimal degree of accountability. More important, before September 11, subpoenas of this relatively unsupervised type were available only in narrow circumstances. A document production order could be used only to obtain the records of a limited class of travel-related businesses (buses, airplanes, and railroads; physical storage facilities; car rental companies; and hotels and motels—but not restaurants). And to get such an order, the FBI was required to certify that the records were sought for a foreign intelligence purpose and that there were specific facts confirming that the records pertained to the agent of a foreign power.[9]

Another device that predates September 11—the national security letter—provides even less accountability. Like a Foreign Intelligence Surveillance Court order, a national security letter allows no opportunity for the affected client to contest the demand and prohibits the recipient from ever revealing to anyone that the records had been sought. But, unlike the relatively unsupervised court order, a national security letter does not receive even cursory review by a judge. Designated FBI officials are given the authority to issue and sign these letters themselves, and thus the letters are subject to no independent oversight whatsoever.

For national security letters, the only limitations before September 11 were two. First, as in the case of a Foreign Intelligence Surveillance Court order, the FBI official was required to certify the foreign intelligence purpose and the existence of specific facts showing that the records pertained to a foreign agent.[10] Second, national security letters, like Foreign Intelligence Surveillance Court orders, could be used to obtain only narrowly defined types of information. The court order gave access to records of travel-related businesses with little judicial oversight, while national security letters, lacking even minimal judicial oversight, were available only to obtain bank records, telephone billing records, and certain credit agency reports.[11] The absence of any external accountability was considered acceptable because of the extraordinary need for secrecy and quick action in national security situations and because only limited kinds of information were exposed to this clandestine regime of unchecked power.

DEVELOPMENTS AFTER SEPTEMBER 11

Although the safeguards of the normal subpoena system had been diluted before September 11, the Patriot Act took three interrelated steps that further reduced privacy and accountability. Their cumulative effect is far-reaching. First, in the specialized statutory regimes governing financial records, educational records, and the like, new counterterrorism exceptions were created, allowing investigators to bypass the normal oversight mechanisms. Second, in the government's least supervised intelligence-gathering regimes—the FISA document production order and the national security letter—threshold requirements were relaxed, making such measures much easier to invoke. Third, these tools were reconfigured to reach a much wider range of information, some of it far more sensitive than anything previously subject to their largely unilateral powers. For the first time, religious liberty, freedom of association, freedom of the press, and freedom of inquiry were directly threatened.

Several provisions of the Patriot Act are implicated in these developments. One of the best known, section 215, is applicable only to Foreign Intelligence Surveillance Court orders; it includes the controversial power to obtain library and bookstore records. Section 505 expands the scope of the national security letter, and section 507 relaxes the specialized safeguards applicable to educational records. Legally, the three sections are distinct. Section 215 is under constitutional attack from several directions, and it sunsets automatically in December 2005. In contrast, section 505, also under constitutional attack, does not sunset. Although one federal court has already held it unconstitutional and enjoined its enforcement,[12] it will remain in effect indefinitely if that decision is overturned or narrowed on appeal. Section 507, the least controversial, does not sunset, and to date it has not faced a constitutional challenge. Yet, the same power-enhancing innovations are important (and troubling) for all three provisions: reduced threshold requirements and much greater scope for the government's least accountable intelligence-gathering tools.

LOWERING THE BAR

Before September 11, Foreign Intelligence Surveillance Court orders and national security letters had an identical threshold requirement: investigators had to certify that the records sought pertained to a suspected foreign agent and that the FBI had specific, objective facts supporting those suspicions.[13] Sections 215 and 505 replace that standard with a new prerequisite, an FBI certificate stating that the records "are *sought for* an authorized investigation . . . to protect against international terrorism."[14] Sections 215 and 505 thus drop both of the pre–September 11 requirements (the suspected status as a foreign agent and the existence of an objective basis for suspicion), replacing them with a condition addressed solely to the investigator's purpose. The FBI is required merely to self-certify that it is acting in good faith.

The difference is important. It is no longer essential for the FBI to have factual support for its decision to investigate, and it is not even necessary for agents to believe that the targeted person is a suspected offender or a foreign agent. Thanks to sections 215 and 505, covered records pertaining to any law-abiding American citizen are available for inspection on a clandestine basis, whenever a field office supervisor has a hunch that the records may advance an investigation of someone else or provide background information relevant to antiterror efforts in general. No doubt, most FBI agents will use common sense in exercising such broad powers. But an accountability mechanism that can be satisfied whenever an agency certifies its own good faith is not a regime of accountability at all.

Reinforcing these changes, section 507 makes confidential education records more accessible even when the government chooses not to invoke its FISA and national security letter authorities. Again, the Patriot Act allows an individual to be targeted even when he or she is not suspected of any wrongdoing or of any link to a foreign agent; the FERPA confidentiality requirements give way whenever a federal official certifies that the records are "likely to contain information . . . relevant to an authorized investigation . . . of domestic or international terrorism."[15] As a result, it is enough for FBI agents to believe that the student's records might help them investigate someone else or provide useful background—for example, insights into the history or philosophy of Islam.[16] The concern is not that the FBI will routinely cast such an absurdly wide net. The problem is that no mechanism is in place to prevent the kinds of "mission creep" and abuse of individuals that occurred at the FBI in the past, before oversight was tightened.

BROADENING THE REACH

The government's least regulated surveillance tools are not only easier to obtain but now give investigators access to a much broader range of information. Before September 11 national security letters were available only for financial data, telephone transaction records, and consumer credit reports, and in theory this remains true today. But Congress has made generous additions to the kinds of information included under these headings. The "financial" heading, for example, now includes all records held by real estate agents, car dealers, travel agencies, insurance companies, and credit card companies, along with records held by "any other business designated by the Secretary [of the Treasury] whose cash transactions have a high degree of usefulness in criminal, tax, or regulatory matters."[17]

Even more important, however, is the dramatic change in the reach of the FISA document production order. Before September 11 investigators could use this tool only when seeking the records of travel-related businesses. As redefined by section 215, the FISA order can now reach documents and records of all kinds. The amended FISA section is still entitled "Certain Business Records," but that caption is now misleading because the provision, unlike its predecessor, is *not* limited to business records. The new provision applies to "any tangible things (including books, records, papers, documents, and other items),"[18] and it was intended to reach every physical item, regardless of its commercial or noncommercial character.

As a result, the FISA document production order can now be used to gain access to customer records, personnel files, and medical reports. It applies to such businesses as credit card companies, HMOs, magazine publishers, booksellers, and video rental stores. And it reaches the files of noncommercial entities of all sorts, including libraries, social clubs, any church or temple or mosque, and political action groups such as the American-Arab Anti-Discrimination Committee, Greenpeace, and the Sierra Club. The Department of Justice even insists that it includes tangible items that are not documents or records at all, such as an apartment key held by a landlord.[19]

Combined with the reduced threshold requirements, these innovations give investigators quick, relatively unsupervised access to highly personal and politically sensitive records. And, despite the Justice Department's repeated, brazenly false denials,[20] the records can pertain to any individual, including law-abiding American citizens not in any way suspected of links to terrorism or to foreign agents.

Beyond requiring that agents act in good faith and believe the records to be relevant, the only limitation is a proviso repeated in each of the amendments: these document production demands cannot be part of "an investigation of a United States person . . . conducted solely on the basis of activities protected by the First Amendment."[21] The proviso sounds reassuring, but it applies only when an investigation is predicated *solely* on protected activities. In practice there are few, if any, investigations that cannot be justified by pointing to some combination of constitutionally protected speech and brief moments of unprotected activity. As the discussion below shows in more detail, the First Amendment proviso is virtually meaningless. The Patriot Act's document production tools are powerful—too powerful to accept without careful consideration of their value.

ASSESSING THE NEW POWERS

The new document production regimes unquestionably put core constitutional liberties at risk. Fourth Amendment privacy rights and First Amendment freedoms of speech and religion are directly endangered. But that fact in itself does not automatically make the expanded powers inadvisable or unconstitutional. Only a close look at the details can determine whether the new approach is truly necessary, whether the constitutional dangers are unavoidable, and which of the new powers, if any, should give way to countervailing civil liberties concerns. In fact, on examination, the new powers prove to be not only dangerous, but much broader than necessary. Several relatively straightforward steps can restore accountability without impeding efficient and effective counterterrorism efforts.

A NEED FOR MORE POWER?

> when clock is ticking ironically is when we might want to not do torture b/c no time for errors

The novel feature of the new document production powers is not that they reach private material that was wholly beyond investigators' reach before September 11. Rather, the effect of the Patriot Act is to make such material accessible more easily and more quickly, with less "red tape."

The need for more streamlined procedures is not apparent at first blush. Documents and records of virtually any kind can be reached through a grand jury subpoena, and subpoenas normally are not difficult to obtain. But logistical and technical problems do arise. To get a grand jury subpoena, an FBI agent must contact a

federal prosecutor, and if a grand jury is not already sitting, the prosecutor must convene one. If the need arises on a weekend, the agent
may have to wait until Monday morning at the earliest, and in rural
areas the wait may be longer. If investigating agents are in New York
and learn that important documents are in Houston, they face an
additional layer of calls and contacts before the subpoena can emerge
from the Houston grand jury. All these steps, of course, have the
feel of utterly pointless technicalities. When the right person finally
gets to the right court, it will be a purely mechanical matter to get the
subpoena signed. Meanwhile, though, the clock is ticking. Hours
that could have been spent on investigation will have been spent on
paperwork instead, and where time is of the essence, as it often is in
terrorism investigations, critical opportunities could conceivably be
lost.

What is hard to determine, however, is whether these kinds of difficulties are largely theoretical or frequent and real. Justice
Department statements defending the Patriot Act systematically
describe, section by section, many actual situations in which various
sections of the act have been used successfully, but for sections 215
and 505 (the document production order and national security letter
provisions) no concrete examples are given. The department's mate-
rials do mention cases in which investigators needed access to library
records and similar documents, but, by its own account, the Justice
Department was able to obtain the necessary records in each instance
by the usual subpoena procedure, *without* having to resort to FISA
court orders or national security letters.

Aggregate statistics are likewise unavailable or uninformative.
The Justice Department long insisted that data on the use of FISA
court orders were too sensitive to be revealed. But, in the face of
widespread concern about FBI snooping into library and business
records, the department finally announced in September 2003 how
often such demands had been made. The number was: zero.[22] Though
meant to reassure the public, the news of complete nonuse—during
two years of intense antiterror efforts—leaves fears about potential
future abuses in place while reinforcing doubt about whether the section 215 powers are really needed. In any event, Justice documents
recently released under court order indicate that section 215 was used
(at least once) just weeks after the announcement of nonuse was
made.[23] Moreover, the department has made extensive use of national
security letters: an ACLU freedom-of-information request produced

a six-page list of national security letters issued since October 2001, with every line of every page blacked out as confidential.[24]

Even those sketchy details shed no light on the questions that matter. Could investigators have taken the same steps without bypassing the safeguards of the prior document order, national security letter, and subpoena regimes? Or were the FISA and national security letter tools available only because of the Patriot Act amendments? If the latter was the case, was there a need to forgo normal subpoena procedures? Or could investigators have respected ordinary accountability measures and still have obtained the same information, without any loss of effectiveness? The potential payoff from reducing "red tape" remains an unproven speculation.

THE LOOMING THREAT TO FIRST AMENDMENT AND FOURTH AMENDMENT RIGHTS

Whatever their value, the new document production regimes threaten several distinct constitutional interests. These regimes govern more than just the mechanics of moving boxes of files. Documents and records reveal intensely private information—finances and travel patterns, medical histories, recordings bought, videos rented, and books borrowed. An investigator's ability to sift through all a citizen's documents and records can be as intrusive (or even more intrusive) than the power to listen in on his or her phone calls. At stake is the central value of the Fourth Amendment, the right to preserve a private space in which people are free to grow, explore, or simply be themselves, what Brandeis called "the right to be let alone—the most comprehensive of rights and the right most valued by civilized men."[25]

First Amendment values—political expression, freedom of association, and religious liberty—are at stake as well. Many Americans believe that they personally have nothing to fear from broad investigative powers, and many of them are probably right. If they follow a mainstream religion, take little interest in politics, and have no desire to criticize government, large corporations, or other powerful institutions, they may not care whether the FBI knows what church they belong to or what consumer products they buy. Greater FBI surveillance powers will not stop them from reading the latest bestseller or doing any of their other daily activities. If such powers make them a little safer from terrorism, they may consider the price trivial and well worth paying. As a Florida woman said, dismissing concerns about the library records powers, "I haven't heard about it, but frankly, I have nothing to hide."[26]

But a healthy democracy depends on its critics and dissenters, even when they are a small minority. If the government can easily discover what books Americans read, where they pray, and what political organizations they join, then the ability to learn about unpopular subjects, support unpopular causes, and practice religion freely is at grave risk.

In 1956 the attorney general of Alabama, in an effort to investigate possible illegal activity by the local chapter of the NAACP, obtained a court order directing the organization to give him copies of its membership lists. The Supreme Court unanimously held that, absent proof of a compelling need for the information, such mandatory disclosure was unconstitutional.[27] The Court stressed the importance of group association for effective advocacy and the importance of confidential affiliation as a means for sustaining unpopular groups. In practice, the Court said, compelled disclosure of membership would discourage groups from speaking out, "dissuade others from joining . . . because of fear of exposure of their beliefs," and result in "unconstitutional intimidation" of the free exercise of constitutional rights.[28]

When government can show a strong need for membership lists and similar information, NAACP v. Alabama and other precedents do permit compulsory disclosure.[29] The Alabama attorney general had insisted that the NAACP membership lists were relevant to his investigation. But when the NAACP moved to quash the subpoena, a trial court took evidence to assess that claim. And the Supreme Court, after holding that such issues require "the closest scrutiny," concluded that the purported relevance was too slender to justify the potential injury to First Amendment rights. In a later case, the Court reached the same conclusion in a national-security context, holding that investigators had insufficient evidence to demand NAACP membership lists for an inquiry into possible Communist infiltration of the civil rights movement.[30] The safeguard of independent judicial scrutiny ensures that legitimate law enforcement needs will be respected while minimizing their potential to arouse public fear and chill the exercise of constitutional rights.

The new document production regimes strike at the heart of this carefully balanced system. Because they avoid normal subpoena procedures, they eliminate any opportunity to seek a judicial inquiry into the circumstances of an investigative demand and the significance of the information sought. They allow compulsory disclosure of an association's members and financial supporters, on nothing more than an investigator's unchallengeable statement that the information either is "relevant to an authorized investigation"[31] or, more tepid yet, merely is "sought for an authorized investigation."[32] Compounding this absence of judicial scrutiny, the FISA and national security letter procedures also foreclose public criticism because they include an automatic gag order: the recipient of a document demand is prohibited from ever revealing the government's actions to the person concerned, to the press, or to anyone else.[33]

Effective congressional oversight is minimal as well. Semiannually, the attorney general must submit to the House and Senate Judiciary Committees a report on the use of FISA document production orders under section 215, but the report need contain nothing more than the total number of orders filed and granted or denied.[34] In the absence of any specifics whatsoever concerning the kinds of "tangible things" requested and the kinds of organizations from which they were sought, such raw totals are thoroughly uninformative.[35] What is worse, in the case of national security letters and educational record demands, the Patriot Act does not provide for any congressional oversight at all.

DISINGENUOUS JUSTICE DEPARTMENT DEFENSES

In an aggressive effort to defend its new document production powers, the Justice Department has insisted on three points: these sections of the Patriot Act have no impact on U.S. citizens and other law-abiding individuals; the provisions merely fine-tune technical details without granting new substantive powers; and they contain specific restrictions to safeguard First Amendment rights. A clear, straightforward assessment of these arguments requires language that, unfortunately, may sound tactless and partisan. The first claim, though often repeated, is an outright falsehood, as the department's spokespersons surely know. The other claims rest on descriptions of the act that are grossly misleading or, again, blatantly false.

Consider first the assertion that the new provisions have no impact on U.S. citizens. Justice Department spokesman Mark Corallo has been particularly emphatic in pressing this point. He has told the press that FISA's library records power "is limited only to foreign intelligence. . . . U.S. citizens cannot be investigated under this act."[36] He has charged that critics are "misleading the public"[37] and "completely wrong" when they suggest that the Patriot Act can target Americans.[38] Similarly, then assistant attorney general Viet Dinh, speaking at the National Press Club in April 2003, explained that section 215 "is not directed at U.S. persons."[39] U.S. Attorney Timothy Burgess testified to the Alaska state legislature that the charge that the FBI can review library records of U.S. citizens is "absolutely not true. . . . It can't be for U.S. citizens."[40]

In a related vein, Corallo has insisted section 215 has no impact on law-abiding individuals. He told the *San Francisco Chronicle* that library and bookstore demands can be made only when the person targeted "is a spy or a member of a terrorist organization,"[41] and he said to the Associated Press that "the law only applies to agents of a foreign power or a member of a terrorist organization."[42]

Yet, the opposing view, which Corallo dismissed as "completely wrong," is absolutely correct, as he himself surely must know. Prior to the Patriot Act, national security letters and FISA document production orders could be used only against foreign agents (including international terrorists). But sections 215, 505, and 507 eliminated that requirement, replacing it with a standard requiring only that the records are likely to be "relevant." Those sections of the Patriot Act do not require suspicion that the target is a foreign agent or a terrorist; rather, they state explicitly that such orders can be used in an "investigation of a United States person."[43] Indeed, the FBI's internal guidance memorandum to field offices openly acknowledges these changes. It notes that the Patriot Act "greatly simplified" the process for obtaining records and that the official seeking such records "is *no longer required* to certify that there are specific and articulable facts giving reason to believe that the information sought pertains to a foreign power, or an agent of a foreign power."[44]

The Justice Department's second line of defense is to argue that the controversies are a tempest in a teapot because all documents and records, including the kinds of information that have occasioned such alarm (library records and the like), were accessible to investigators even before the Patriot Act. The new procedures, the department maintains, merely adjust technical details. Thus, in a lengthy document seeking to debunk civil liberties criticism ("The USA Patriot Act: Myth vs. Reality"), the Department of Justice states that "obtaining business records is a long-standing law enforcement tactic," that "grand juries for years have issued subpoenas to all manner of businesses, including libraries . . . ," and that "Section 215 authorized the FISA court to issue similar orders in national security investigations."[45] Similarly, in a letter to the House Judiciary Committee, the department insists that "Congress did not authorize a new innovation with section 215."[46] In other words, the provisions do not create any new powers to intrude on citizens' privacy.

What the new provisions do, however, is to obliterate the oversight that subpoena procedures afford to protect against government overreaching and abuse. To insist that dismantling of oversight mechanisms works no change of substance is, in effect, to argue that because homeowners are already subject to search pursuant to a judicial warrant, these citizens lose no significant privacy if police are instead allowed to search a private home on nothing more than their own certificate that they are acting in good faith. To treat oversight mechanisms as irrelevant red tape is to assume away any need for accountability and to trivialize the kinds of procedural safeguards that are central to the Bill of Rights.

Some Justice Department efforts to defend section 215 seem to recognize that procedures matter but then argue that the section 215 procedures are equivalent to those in place before September 11. Corallo has told the press that to check on a person's reading habits, the FBI must have "credible evidence"[47] or "probable cause that the person [targeted] is a terrorist or a foreign spy."[48] He asserts that the "standard of proof [is] the same as it's always been. It's not been lessened."[49] Similarly, an FBI spokeswoman told the *San Francisco Chronicle* that criticism of the Patriot Act was the product of "hysteria" and stated that "we still have to show probable cause for any actions we take."[50]

To support its argument that threshold requirements are unchanged, the Justice Department once again must resort to claims that are patently false. Document demands under sections 215, 505, and 507 do not require probable cause, and they do not require the evidentiary support that was necessary before September 11.[51] Prior to the Patriot Act, Foreign Intelligence Surveillance Court orders and national security letters required the FBI to certify that it had "specific and articulable facts" supporting its suspicions that the target was a foreign agent. But as the Justice Department's own internal memorandums acknowledge,[52] suspicion relating to the target is no longer necessary, and the slender requirement that remains (relevance to the investigation) does not need to be supported by any representation about the facts, if any, behind the investigator's conclusions.[53]

In a related effort to claim that section 215 retains meaningful safeguards, Justice Department officials repeatedly state that agents can obtain a FISA order only when they can "convince a judge" of the need for it[54] or "demonstrate" that the records are sought for a legitimate purpose.[55] Again, the claims are simply not true. Whenever an FBI official files the required certificate of relevance, section 215 provides that the Foreign Intelligence Surveillance Court judge "shall" issue the order requested. The FBI is not required to set forth its evidence or its reasoning, and the judge is granted no power to question the basis for the FBI assertions. The judge *must* issue the order, whether "convinced" or not.

As its third line of defense for section 215, Justice Department officials insist that this section has "a narrow scope that scrupulously respects First Amendment rights."[56] Spokeswoman Barbara Comstock protests that "section 215 goes to great lengths to preserve the First Amendment rights of libraries, bookstores, . . . and their patrons."[57] The department's "Myth vs. Reality" report claims that "Section 215 expressly protects the First Amendment,"[58] and Comstock adds, "FBI agents are prohibited from using a suspect's exercise of First Amendment rights as a pretext for seeking records or information."[59]

These claims extravagantly exaggerate the import of statutory language stating merely that a section 215 order cannot be sought for an "investigation of a United States person . . . conducted solely on the basis of activities protected by the first amendment. . . ."[60] Far from ensuring "scrupulous" protection, going to "great lengths," or prohibiting inquiries based on dubious pretexts, the First Amendment caveat is virtually meaningless. It offers no protection at all to foreign travelers in the United States (a Canadian tourist, for example). More important, an investigation of a U.S. citizen can be conducted partly or even primarily on the basis of advocacy, religious affiliation, or political associations, provided that investigators can justify their suspicions by referencing some combination of constitutionally protected speech and unprotected activity.

Suppose, for example, that the fiery sermon of a radical Islamic cleric arouses an FBI agent's suspicions. The agent would seldom think (much less acknowledge) that he or she was launching an investigation *solely* on the basis of constitutionally protected speech.

Almost inevitably, there will be some suspicious-looking shreds of information about the cleric's nonpolitical, nonreligious activities. At that point the investigation would not be based on speech alone. Even if there were no information beyond the speech itself, the agent's decision to investigate presumably would reflect suspicion that the speaker intended to aid or encourage acts of violence. In such a case, under existing law, the speech itself can lose its First Amendment shelter.[61]

Even if FBI actions of that sort prove to be rare (and of course there is no guarantee that they will be), the potential for such investigations will chill religious freedom and have powerfully corrosive effects on democratic debate and political dissent. Some of these effects are already evident. In Michigan and Oregon, Muslim community organizations report that "attendance at prayer services, educational forums and social events has substantially dropped" and that donations are almost half of what they were before passage of the Patriot Act.[62] In Tennessee, an agency of the Church World Service, one of the leading Protestant umbrella organizations for refugee relief, has noted that some immigrants are afraid to turn to it for assistance, and it has changed its record-keeping procedures in order to protect the personal information of donors.[63]

These concerns are at the heart of two important constitutional challenges. In *Muslim Community Association of Ann Arbor v. Ashcroft*,[64] litigation currently pending, the plaintiffs argue that section 215 violates the Fourth Amendment prohibition of unreasonable searches and First Amendment protections for religious and political affiliation. They object in particular to the section 215 power to obtain records from political and religious groups without meaningful judicial oversight and to the gag rule that automatically—without any independent determination of a need for secrecy—prevents the affected organizations from ever revealing the government demand for documents to anyone.

The second case, *Doe v. Ashcroft*,[65] involves a section 505 national security letter seeking customer transaction records from an Internet service provider. The records sought do not involve the most sensitive First Amendment concerns, those centered on religious affiliation and political advocacy, but because the government invoked the national security letter, the demand lacks even the minimal judicial supervision that accompanies a section 215 FISA order. In *Doe*, the federal district court held section 505 unconstitutional on several interrelated grounds.[66] The absence of judicial oversight, even when there is no determination of a need for speed or secrecy, the court ruled, violates the constitutional prohibition of unreasonable search, and the gag order violates freedom of speech. Courts will almost certainly have even greater difficulty accepting the section 215 regime for FISA document production orders to libraries, bookstores, religious associations, and political advocacy groups. But even if the FISA and national security letters powers can survive constitutional challenge, Congress clearly should take a close look at ways to narrow these powers in order to meet legitimate law enforcement needs without threatening Fourth Amendment and First Amendment interests.

ADMINISTRATIVE SUBPOENAS: SHOULD CONGRESS PERMIT EVEN LESS ACCOUNTABILITY?

For the moment, many members of Congress seem less interested in restoring accountability than in granting the FBI even stronger powers to obtain information. A recent House bill, the Antiterrorism Tools Enhancement Act, and a parallel Senate proposal, would authorize the FBI to compel the production of documents, records, and any "other tangible things" by issuing an "administrative subpoena."[67] This device, like a national security letter, is a document production order issued and signed by a Justice Department official without any judicial involvement at all, and it includes provision for a similar gag order, barring the recipient from disclosing the document demand to anyone other than his or her attorney.

The proposed administrative subpoena would, however, be considerably broader than the national security letter. Unlike national security letters, which currently are available only for telephone and Internet records, financial transactions, and credit reports, the new administrative subpoena would reach any records whatsoever, including library borrowings, bookstore purchases, and the membership lists of political and religious associations. In effect, the administrative subpoena power would be comparable to the controversial document production orders now available under section 215, but it would be even broader in three important respects. The new administrative subpoena would be available for domestic as well as international terrorism investigations. As currently drafted, it would not carry even the weak First Amendment safeguard that applies to section 215. Finally, the minimal judicial oversight built into section 215—the

requirement of a Foreign Intelligence Surveillance Court order—
would be eliminated entirely.* Librarians, Muslim community organizations, and others troubled by the broad reach of section 215
would come to see that provision as comparatively tame when mea-
sured against the powers conferred by the proposed Antiterrorism
Tools Enhancement Act.

As in its efforts to defend section 215, Justice Department arguments for a broad administrative subpoena regime obscure the large
increase in powers that the proposal would entail. The department
emphasizes that grand jury subpoenas already reach all records that
would be subject to an administrative subpoena.[68] But the grand jury
procedure provides greater opportunities for oversight by the court
and by a federal prosecutor with some independence from the FBI.[69]

The Justice Department also notes that administrative subpoena
authority already exists in investigations of Medicare fraud, securities
fraud, and several other regulatory violations. It is absurd, the department argues, to confer such powers for investigations of routine economic offenses but not for efforts to combat terrorism.[70] The
difference, however, is that Medicare and securities investigations,
by definition, target highly regulated activity that enjoys no constitutional protection; they almost never implicate sensitive records such
as bookstore purchases and religious membership lists. Equally important, regulatory investigations typically seek records from the individual or firm that is under suspicion, and as a result the subpoena
recipient is in a position to challenge improper demands and ensure
an opportunity for judicial oversight. No such accountability procedures are available for the proposed administrative subpoenas, which
almost inevitably will be directed to third-party entities having little
or no incentive to bring oversight mechanisms into play.

Congress must understand that the existing FISA and national security letter authorities already make dangerous inroads on ordinary First
Amendment and Fourth Amendment safeguards. The FBI does not need
even greater insulation from oversight. Rather, congressional efforts

---

*Judicial review would be available if the recipient of an administrative subpoena
moved to quash it prior to compliance. But in the typical terrorism investigation, the
records sought will pertain to some other individual, and the subpoena recipient will
be barred from informing that person or discussing the subpoena with him in any way.
As a result, the recipient will almost always comply, without undertaking the expense
of challenging the subpoena on behalf of the individual who is actually affected.

should be directed toward reestablishing reasonable mechanisms of accountability that will protect constitutional rights without hampering legitimate counterterrorism efforts.

SOLUTIONS

The central flaw in the new document production regimes is their dangerous and unnecessary erosion of accountability. The path for reform follows directly from that diagnosis. Accountability should be restored in several, mutually reinforcing ways in order to guarantee the appropriate use of these sensitive powers.

CONGRESSIONAL OVERSIGHT

The first step is to require strong congressional oversight. No matter what the circumstances of urgency or complexity in a national security investigation, the simple expedient of after-the-fact statistical reporting to Congress poses no conceivable danger of interference or inconvenience. This minimal safeguard is essentially costless and should not be controversial.

Yet, none of the major reform bills introduced in the 108th Congress included significant new reporting obligations for the government's sweeping document production powers.[71] FISA stipulates that the attorney general must give Congress a semiannual report indicating the number of document orders obtained under section 215, but the law does not require disclosure of any further details.[72] The Intelligence Reform Act of 2004 modestly enlarged the prescribed reporting for electronic surveillance and physical searches, but its only provision applicable to documents simply restates the preexisting duty to disclose semiannually the aggregate number of section 215 orders.[73] Under the 2004 act, the Justice Department also must report the number of times that information acquired under FISA was approved for use in a criminal prosecution,[74] and that aggregate number might include cases involving information obtained through section 215. But the intelligence reform legislation does not mandate disclosure of whether any section 215 cases actually are included in the total and, if so, how many of them—details that are essential for oversight. Further, the law does not call for any reports at all relating to the use of national security letters and educational records orders.

Congress should require for all three of these regimes a semiannual report including not only the total number of orders issued but also, at a minimum, such essential details as:

- the nature of the entity from which the items were sought, and in particular the number sought from charities, political organizations, religious organizations and their affiliates, libraries, bookstores, video stores.

- the nature of the "tangible things" sought, in particular the number of orders that sought financial statements, communication records, employment files, membership rosters, contribution lists, medical histories, and educational records.

- a breakdown of the number of times that information obtained from documents in each category was approved for use in a criminal prosecution and for what kinds of offenses; and

- the number of arrests and convictions for each type of offense obtained as a result of each type of document production power.

PUBLIC ACCOUNTABILITY

A second important step is to eliminate the sweeping gag order that now accompanies all national security letters and FISA document demands. It might seem that this step is neither simple nor costless because there are circumstances in which an investigation requires assurance that the target will not be alerted. But that perfectly legitimate need can easily be addressed on a case-by-case basis. For that reason, one federal court has already ruled that the automatic, indefinite gag provisions of existing law are unconstitutional.[75] Even the Justice Department's own proposal for administrative subpoenas seeks authority for a gag order only when the attorney general certifies the need for it in a particular case. That proposal also would grant the subpoena recipient the right to have the gag order lifted as soon as circumstances permit. A similar, well-tailored measure should replace the across-the-board prohibitions on notifying subjects of investigation currently attached to sections 215 and 505.

SUBSTANTIVE BOUNDARIES

However effective congressional oversight and public disclosure may prove to be, there is no substitute for judicial oversight on a case-by-case basis. But such oversight is now for practical purposes impossible because the only threshold requirement for a document demand is the FBI's self-certification that it is acting in good faith. To avoid overreaching and to restore a meaningful, independent check, it is essential to limit these demands to the records of individuals linked to terrorist activity.

There is no persuasive reason for sections 215 and 505 to have wider reach. For those rare cases in which there is legitimate need to obtain records of individuals who are not suspects themselves, the grand jury subpoena remains available and can readily be tailored to the circumstances. Indeed, the Justice Department's own defense of sections 215 and 505 emphasizes that "the law only applies to agents of a foreign power or a member of a terrorist organization."[76] Those sections should now be brought into line with Justice's characterization of them.

There is likewise no persuasive objection to restoring the pre–September 11 requirement that the FBI certify having *specific and articulable facts* to support its suspicions against the person whose records are sought. This is the familiar legal formula for describing something more than a purely subjective hunch. Even in today's security-conscious world, fishing expeditions into sensitive documents will hinder rather than promote effective law enforcement and detract from the effort to produce useful intelligence. Good investigators undoubtedly base their actions on objective facts, and it is worthwhile to make clear that sensitive document demands should not be issued otherwise.

JUDICIAL OVERSIGHT

A harder question is whether an FBI certificate alleging specific and articulable facts should be conclusive or whether instead that assertion should be subject to judicial review. A central premise of the

Fourth Amendment is that a police officer's good-faith determination of the facts is not sufficient to justify a search or a similar intrusion into privacy. That principle normally applies to FISA searches and surveillance as well. An independent judicial mind must pass on the existence of probable cause or objective suspicions.[77]

Prior to September 11, FISA document production orders and national security letters were issued without independent judicial review; the FBI certificate was conclusive. But those powers applied only to records held by travel businesses, telephone companies, and banks—all situations in which expectations of privacy are relatively low and the potential for interference with political association and religious liberty is virtually nonexistent.

It would be reasonable to preserve that approach, if library records and similarly sensitive documents were excluded altogether from the reach of national security letters and FISA document production orders. In that event, however, the grand jury subpoena process would have to be deployed whenever such documents were needed, at some considerable inconvenience to investigators and with no guarantee that privacy and First Amendment rights would be better protected. When the institution holding sensitive records is not willing or able to challenge the scope of the grand jury subpoena, that process would, if anything, afford less accountability than a FISA framework, especially one involving independent judicial review of the asserted "specific and articulable facts."

A preferable approach, therefore, would be to amend section 215 or replace it (when it sunsets) with a requirement that a Foreign Intelligence Surveillance Court judge determine the sufficiency of the supporting facts. Alternatively, the requirement of an independent judicial determination could be reserved for FISA orders involving certain categories of especially sensitive information, such as medical reports, educational files, and of course all records touching establishments and organizations at the core of First Amendment activity (libraries, bookstores, video stores, religious organizations, and political advocacy groups).

The latter approach, with a distinct standard for particular types of data, would be a bit more elaborate to draft, but it would appropriately focus attention on the kinds of records for which close judicial oversight is most needed. As the Supreme Court held in *NAACP v. Alabama* and similar cases,[78] document demands touching on core rights of political and religious association require careful judicial scrutiny of the investigator's legitimate needs and the alternative means available to meet them. Similarly, although reporters have no absolute privilege to shield the identity of their sources, the courts typically insist that prosecutors attempt first to obtain the needed information by other means, in order to reduce the potential chilling effect on freedom of the press.[79]

To bring the new document powers into line with these principles, a revised FISA procedure should make clear that, in assessing the basis for issuing a document production order, the judge should take heavily into account the nature of the items sought. In the case of especially sensitive records, unless unusual circumstances dictate otherwise, the judge should be directed to apply *NAACP v. Alabama* standards, scrutinizing the proposed order to ensure that the records sought are important (not merely "relevant") to the investigation and that alternative ways to obtain the information are explored, in order to minimize the threat to First Amendment rights.

A discriminating approach of this sort, insisting on oversight and accountability where feasible, can go a long way toward restoring public trust in the integrity of national security investigations, without frustrating well-focused and effective intelligence-gathering efforts.

Chapter 5

ENHANCED POWERS IN CONVENTIONAL LAW ENFORCEMENT

The regime governing conventional law enforcement surveillance before September 11 was a complex mixture of stringent limitations, broad powers, and awkward compromises. In the atmosphere of irresistible demands for stronger law enforcement that followed, the Patriot Act shifted this balance in the direction of greatly expanded investigative powers—including powers to investigate crimes entirely unrelated to terrorism.

Seventeen distinct provisions address search and surveillance matters in conventional law enforcement. Of these, eleven simply correct technical oversights and anomalies in prior law, without posing any new dangers to individual privacy. But six (in addition to the important Foreign Intelligence Surveillance Act amendments discussed in Chapters 3 and 4) do raise significant privacy concerns—provisions, for example, that authorize clandestine physical searches and expanded surveillance of electronic mail. The act draws a distinction between these sections, providing that some sunset automatically in December 2005, but that others do not. Oddly, there is little correspondence between the most problematic provisions and those that were selected to sunset. One relatively technical matter, concerning the nationwide effectiveness of search warrants, is dealt with in two very similar sections, one of which sunsets and one of which does not. A majority of the technical provisions (seven of the eleven) are listed to sunset automatically, while most of the important and controversial provisions (five of the six) will not.

79

This chapter discusses the more technical items briefly and explains why none of them should be considered controversial. But first it considers in detail the six provisions that do raise significant privacy concerns. These measures offer some potential advantages, but they have provoked considerable unease, and many critics insist that they are not worth their costs.

The value of more information, of course, is not boundless. As explained in Chapter 2, information is costly. A selective approach to new surveillance powers is essential to preserve core freedoms, to reduce the dangers of government abuse, to enhance the perceived fairness and legitimacy of surveillance operations, and, perhaps most important, to give law enforcement cost-effective tools that can deliver genuine security benefits. At least three of the more significant provisions are seriously flawed, and there should be a strong bipartisan consensus on the need to pursue their objectives in less intrusive or more tightly regulated ways.

CLANDESTINE PHYSICAL SEARCHES (SECTION 213)

When police search a home or business, they ordinarily must knock and announce their purpose before entering, and they must give the property owner a copy of the warrant so that the person searched knows exactly what authority the police have and what, if anything, they are allowed to seize.[1] These requirements help minimize the fear and intimidation a search provokes and help ensure that the police will not exceed the bounds of their authority, for instance, by rummaging through all drawers, closets, and personal papers in a wide "fishing expedition." Ordinarily, any failure to follow the notification requirements will render the search "unreasonable" and therefore illegal under the Fourth Amendment.

Nonetheless, Fourth Amendment law has long recognized exceptions to these requirements when notice would expose officers to danger or risk the destruction of evidence. In drug investigations, for example, a particular suspect might resist by force or eliminate all traces of drug activity as soon as the police announce their presence; where there is an objective basis for such fears, courts can issue a "no-knock" warrant authorizing police to execute a surprise entry.[2] A similar, though far less common, problem arises when the entry and search must be completely surreptitious, so that the occupants do not realize they are under suspicion. In that situation, courts sometimes permit a so-called sneak-and-peek search, in which the warrant authorizes police to enter and leave while occupants are away from home, waiting several days before giving the property owner notice and a copy of the warrant. The case law makes clear, however, that no-knock and sneak-and-peek searches are reserved for unusual circumstances and must kept within narrow bounds. Prior to September 11, courts had developed detailed prerequisites for no-knock warrants, but few cases had examined the comparatively rare sneak-and-peek situations.

Section 213 of the Patriot Act adds to federal law a provision that for the first time gives statutory authority for clandestine intrusions in domestic law enforcement. It allows a sneak-and-peek search—officially known as a "delayed notice" search—whenever three loosely worded requirements are met. First, the court issuing the warrant must find "reasonable cause" to believe that immediate notice "may have an adverse result." Second, the delayed notice warrant must authorize *only* a search. Normally, no tangible property can be seized, but there is a broad exception to this requirement—the warrant can allow both the search and a seizure whenever the court finds "reasonable necessity." Third, the property owner must get notice of the search "within a reasonable period." Compounding the danger of these vague safeguards, the law defines "an adverse result" in the broadest terms, ranging from danger to life and intimidation of witnesses through flight from prosecution and any other result "seriously jeopardizing an investigation or unduly delaying a trial."[3] And section 213 departs in two additional ways from the principle of narrow tailoring: the new sneak-and-peek power is not limited to terrorism investigations, and it does not sunset automatically.

With its sinister name and slender safeguards, the sneak and peek search has alarmed civil liberties groups and many libertarian conservatives, including prominent Republican members of Congress. In 2003, Representative C. L. Otter (R-Idaho) won strong support for a bill that in effect would have prohibited all delayed notice searches, regardless of circumstances; it passed in the House on a solid 309 to 118 roll call vote.[4] In fact, the authority conferred by section 213 is neither as new nor as radical as its opponents suggest. Yet, it is broader than prior law, broader than necessary, and almost entirely unrelated to fighting terrorism. Delayed notice searches have a place in law enforcement, but Congress must act to ensure that this easily abused tactic remains subject to sufficient controls.

THE IMPACT OF SECTION 213

Prior to September 11, courts had recognized the need for a delayed notice search in a number of situations. For example, in an ongoing investigation of an amphetamines lab, police may need to observe the lab and seek clues on the site to identify its suppliers without alerting them that they are under suspicion.[5] Similarly, when agents authorized to conduct electronic surveillance need to enter a house to install a bug, it would defeat the purpose of the surveillance if the target were immediately notified that a bug had been installed; covert entry is essential.[6] In situations like these, magistrates often authorized searches with delayed notification; in 1984 the FBI reported having conducted thirty-four clandestine searches, mostly in terrorism and narcotics cases, though one was in a kidnapping case.[7] Appellate courts upheld these delayed notice warrants,[8] but there were only a handful of decisions, and the criteria they specified for a valid sneak and peek were not identical.

On the threshold question of whether clandestine entry is permissible at all, decisions handed down before September 2001 alternatively said that secrecy is justified when it is "essential"[9] or "necessary"[10] or simply based on a "good reason."[11] On the question of how long the search may be kept secret, courts agreed that notice normally must be given within seven days, but some allowed extensions of the seven-day period upon "a fresh showing of the need,"[12] while others allowed extensions only upon "a strong showing of necessity."[13] None of the pre–September 11 decisions allowed the clandestine seizure of tangible property, and some said explicitly that a valid delayed notice warrant must explicitly prohibit such seizure.[14]

In addition to these limited powers available in domestic law enforcement, the law before September 2001 provided much broader sneak-and-peek authority, with comparatively few safeguards, in foreign intelligence investigations. Under FISA, the Foreign Intelligence Surveillance Court could authorize repeated clandestine physical searches over extended periods of time with no notice given to the target at all—ever. The only significant prerequisite was that there be probable cause to believe that the target was the agent of a foreign power or international terrorist group.[15] That requirement, however, is far easier to meet than the traditional probable cause and necessity showings required for a domestic sneak and peek both before and after the Patriot Act.

Against this background of judicial standards as they stood before September 11, section 213 cannot be considered a radical innovation, but two points are clear. First, it does next to nothing to assist in the battle against international terrorism, because the FBI already had (and still has) even broader power to conduct sneak-and-peek searches under FISA. And second, it adds substantially to government's clandestine search powers in conventional crime cases. For domestic law enforcement, section 213 weakens in every respect the safeguards that courts had developed before September 11.

Consider first the threshold prerequisites for a clandestine domestic search. Earlier decisions described them in slightly different terms, but the most flexible standard required either "reasonable necessity" or "good reason for delay." Section 213 replaces those tests with one that requires only reasonable cause to believe that immediate notice "may have" just about any adverse effect, including "seriously jeopardizing" an investigation or "unduly delaying" a trial.[16] Yet, there is almost always a risk that immediate notification "may" jeopardize an investigation, and jeopardy to an investigation almost always implies difficulties collecting evidence and therefore a possible need to delay the trial.

Likewise, in setting the permissible delay before giving notice, section 213 replaces the clear, seven-day norm under prior law with authority to delay notification for "a reasonable period." Extensions, previously allowed only on a "fresh showing" or "strong showing" of necessity, can be granted whenever there is "good cause." Worse, the seizure of tangible property, strongly disfavored previously, is allowed whenever "reasonably necessary." Though courts could give these terms a demanding interpretation, section 213, as written, adopts in each of these respects a standard even looser and vaguer than the least demanding of the requirements under prior law.

The Department of Justice has used its broad section 213 powers with some frequency.[17] During a recent eighteen-month period, the department made forty-seven requests for sneak-and-peek warrants and received court approval every time. It also received approval for fourteen of its fifteen requests for delayed notification of a seizure. The postponement most commonly authorized was for seven days, but courts granted delays for as long as ninety days, and some allowed delays of "unspecified duration lasting until the indictment was unsealed." Moreover, the department sought 248 extensions of an initial delay (including multiple requests in the same case) and received approval every time. By Justice's own admission, the cases involved a wide range of criminal conduct, from international terrorism (where a FISA sneak and peek would have been available anyway) to domestic terrorism to activity with no terrorism component at all, including trafficking in drugs and child pornography.[18] There is little justification for leaving in place such vague limits on this particularly intrusive and disconcerting governmental power in law enforcement areas with slender or nonexistent connections to the "war on terrorism."

SOLUTIONS

Among the many sneak-and-peek proposals now before Congress, one would subject section 213 to sunset on December 31, 2005;[19] one would simply repeal it (thus restoring the prior standards);[20] the Otter amendment would in effect prohibit delayed notice searches altogether;[21] and several other bills would restrict these searches to especially dangerous situations, require notice within seven days (with the possibility of extensions), or require the attorney general to issue regular public reports concerning all requests for delayed notification.[22]

In considering this problem, Congress should first have clearly in mind that the delayed notification search is a technique of conventional law enforcement and that it seldom if ever needs to be invoked in the battle against international terrorism. For international investigations, FISA grants far broader power to conduct clandestine searches and seizures, and it imposes no obligation ever to notify the affected property owner or the target of the search, unless a criminal prosecution ensues. As a result, section 213 is simply not a relevant part of the response to September 11; it deals with an unrelated problem.

For that reason, outright repeal of section 213 is not an irresponsible proposal. Nonetheless, now that Congress has ventured into this area and recognized the somewhat discordant standards of prior law, an attempt to fix the problem wisely seems far preferable to simply abandoning the legislative effort.

That consideration also suggests that limiting section 213 powers to the investigation of terrorism cases, as several of the pending bills propose,[23] is not as attractive an option as it might first appear. In non-terrorism cases, that approach would have the effect of either barring delayed notice searches completely or restoring the stricter but somewhat inconsistent standards of pre–September 11 law. Neither outcome seems ideal. Delayed notice searches are essential when planting a properly authorized electronic bug and can be legitimately justified in other law enforcement situations. Since the section 213 standards must in any event be tightened for domestic terrorism investigations, it seems much better to carry the improvements over to the other circumstances in which delayed notification is an appropriate tactic.

With that in mind, Congress should be prepared to rework section 213 in four important respects. First, the threshold standard for issuing a delayed notice warrant should be higher and far more specific than section 213's requirement of "reasonable cause to believe that providing immediate notification . . . may have an adverse result."[24] Instead, courts should be required to find probable cause to believe that immediate notice would endanger a person's life or safety or would present a substantial risk of flight from prosecution or destruction of evidence (either by the immediate targets of the search or by any of their confederates). Second, the same probable cause finding should be required to support a delayed notice warrant for the seizure of tangible property. Moreover, the delayed notice warrant should require that notification be given within seven days of the search, and courts should be able to authorize extensions or longer initial periods only on a "strong showing of necessity."[25] Finally, as proposed in several bills,[26] the attorney general should be directed to issue regular public reports concerning all requests for delayed notification.

INTERNET SURVEILLANCE: MONITORING SOURCE AND DESTINATION ADDRESSES ("PEN REGISTER" AND "TRAP/TRACE") (SECTION 216)

A pen register is a device that records the telephone numbers dialed from a suspect's phone, and trap-and-trace mechanisms record the numbers from which incoming calls originate. Until September 11 the law prohibited use of these instruments without a court order, but the standard for issuing the order was hardly exacting—the investigator merely had to certify to the court "that the information likely to be obtained . . . is relevant to an ongoing criminal investigation."[27] This test is far less rigorous than the "probable cause" required for search or wiretap, and the court is required to accept the certificate of relevance at face value; it cannot independently assess the objective basis for that assertion as it is required to do when agents claim probable cause for a search. Pen-register and trap/trace orders were permitted even when the target was not a suspect in the investigation, and, unlike surveillance and searches under a traditional warrant, the investigator was not required to report to the court on the results obtained. The lesser safeguards were justified on the premise that these devices record relatively nonprivate information and do not reveal the content of calls or the identity of the participants.

Section 216 of the Patriot Act extends the definition of pen-register and trap/trace information, previously restricted to telephone numbers,[28] to include analogous information that identifies the origin or destination of e-mail and Internet browsing, specifically "routing, addressing, and signaling information."[29] Although the new definition specifically excludes "the contents of any communication" (presumably the subject line and body of a message), it implies that pen-register and trap/trace powers do reach user and subject-matter information embedded in the Internet routing details.

These changes are potentially significant because routing information for e-mail, Web surfing, and Internet search terms can reveal far more about subject matter and the identity of participants than a mere telephone number does. The identity of a Web site, for example, can be as content-specific as the titles of books borrowed from a library or movies rented from a video store. Internet search terms can be even more revealing. For that reason, many prominent privacy advocates forcefully criticize section 216. The privacy concerns are compounded by section 216's clear departure from the principle of narrow tailoring: its powers are not limited to terrorism investigations, and they do not sunset automatically. But it also introduces one safeguard that prior law does not afford for telephone pen registers: the government must keep a detailed log of its Internet monitoring and must provide all the required information to the court within thirty days after the expiration of the monitoring order.

Section 216's overall effects are debatable, with some observers arguing that it actually *enhances* Internet privacy. The debate is usually cast in terms accessible only to those conversant with the arcane specifics of statutes and cybertechnology. But everyone who uses a computer has an interest in understanding this problem.

THE IMPACT OF SECTION 216

The effect of section 216 depends on the way origin and destination identifiers were treated under prior law, and that was, to say the least, far from clear or consistent. In the case of letters sent through the post office, strangers can observe the destination and return addresses that are readily legible on the outside of the envelope, and therefore courts have long held that there is no "reasonable expectation of privacy" for such information. Accordingly, it cannot qualify for Fourth Amendment protection, and Congress has provided no statutory safeguards. As a result, FBI agents need no court order to conduct surveillance aimed at collecting addresses on letters in the mail.

In 1979 the Supreme Court ruled that telephone numbers should be treated just like addresses on an envelope and therefore should be given no Fourth Amendment protection. Unrealistically, the Court concluded that there was no reasonable expectation of privacy in the numbers dialed because the telephone user had "voluntarily conveyed numerical information to the telephone company and 'exposed' that information *to its equipment.*"[30] Congress responded to this artificial analysis by giving telephone numbers statutory protection, requiring a court order (though not probable cause) prior to installation of a pen-register or trap/trace device.

With the advent of e-mail, a gap in this legal regime became apparent because an e-mail "exposes" to the service provider's equipment not only the origin and destination identifiers but the entire content of the message. Under the Supreme Court's reasoning, neither the addresses nor the content would qualify for constitutional protection. Messages conveyed by telephone or by letter would be protected, but messages sent by e-mail would not be. Congress moved to correct this anomaly by requiring strict Title III statutory safeguards (probable cause, a warrant, and minimization procedures) prior to any search for the *content* of an Internet communication.

Oddly, however, Congress did not update its definition of a "pen register," which technically remained tied to the concept of telephone numbers. As a result, e-mail content was tightly protected by Title III, and telephone routing data (phone numbers) were loosely protected by the pen-register provisions, but e-mail routing information fell into a kind of limbo. If considered "content," it would qualify for strict Title III protections; if considered a new form of "telephone number," it would qualify for the looser, mid-level protections of the pen-register provisions. But if it was neither, it would have no statutory or constitutional protection at all. In that case, under obsolete statutory language, information that is more private than a telephone number would have far less legal protection. Not only government agents but also any private party would be free to conduct unrestricted snooping for the origin and destination of anyone's e-mail.

This legal puzzle remained unresolved throughout the 1990s. In July 2000 the Clinton administration proposed a fix that would (like section 216) have extended the pen-register approach to e-mail and Internet addresses. That effort stalled in Congress, but meanwhile the Justice Department assumed that mid-level pen-register protections applied anyway. The department could have argued that e-mail routing information was completely unprotected. But that approach would not help the government as much as one might think. The surveillance legislation not only protects certain kinds of communications data but also obliges private firms to release that data to the government when the statutory procedures are met. If e-mail routing information is not covered by the statute at all, the FBI would have no means to compel an Internet service provider (ISP) to report it to the government, and many ISPs would not do so voluntarily because of the privacy commitments they make to their subscribers. As a result, investigators would have only two choices: they could either hope for ISP cooperation, an uncertain prospect at best, or undertake the cumbersome task of attempting to intercept the information by tapping directly into the Internet themselves. Neither option is satisfactory in practice. Indeed, in November 2000, a federal magistrate in San Jose (home to many major ISPs) apparently precipitated a minor crisis by ruling that there was no statutory pen-register mechanism and thus no basis for issuing an address-monitoring order to an ISP. Other federal magistrates apparently considered the pen-register regime available. There the matter stood on September 11, 2001.

What then is the effect of section 216? Many of its critics assume that it created new government surveillance powers—that before its passage, Internet routing information could not be seized at all or could be seized pursuant only to a demanding Title III warrant.[31] It seems unlikely, however, that the Supreme Court ultimately would have taken that view, and as a matter of practice, the Justice Department was routinely using the telephone pen-register regime for surveillance of e-mail and Internet addresses. If that regime was ultimately held inapplicable (as one federal magistrate had ruled), Internet routing information probably would have been left with no protection at all. The most likely effect of section 216, therefore, was either to restate the law as it stood before or to extend a new, though loose, regime of legal protection to information that previously had none.

Against this complex background, section 216 cannot fairly be painted as an overreaction to September 11 or as an extreme governmental power grab. Indeed, it is notable that section 216 preserves the basic structure of preexisting surveillance law and provides a fairly narrow fix for a difficult technical problem. That said, one might reasonably question whether that hasty fix is the best Congress can offer for a problem that has large implications for Internet privacy. Because e-mail and Internet addresses can reveal so much about the user's interests and activities, safeguards going beyond those of section 216 clearly should be considered.

SOLUTIONS

The pen-register and trap/trace authorities could be narrowed from several directions. Restrictions might, for example, depend on the kind of crime under investigation, the type of communication under surveillance, the scope of judicial oversight, or the showing required to authorize the surveillance.

One possible approach would be to limit the new pen-register and trap/trace powers to terrorism cases. The Justice Department acknowledges that it has used section 216 in investigations of drug distribution, ordinary theft, and other misconduct unrelated to terrorism.[32] Congress could require stricter procedures (such as the Title III wiretap safeguards) in the case of Internet address monitoring not tied to a terrorism investigation.

Similarly, Congress might consider whether it is time to extend the stricter Title III wiretap safeguards to *telephone* pen registers as well. In practice, a telephone pen register reveals significantly more information than the "voluntarily exposed" telephone number. By recording that a phone call was made from a given location, the pen register reveals that someone was present inside that location, often a home, and the length of the call.[33] Yet, in several cases decided subsequent to its 1979 pen-register ruling, the Supreme Court has held that full Fourth Amendment safeguards apply to the use of any technical device that reveals a person's presence in a residence or any information (however limited) about activity within it.[34] Seen through the lens of these subsequent decisions, the reasoning of the 1979 ruling may no longer suffice to justify unregulated pen-register and trap/trace telephone monitoring, at least when the number under surveillance is located in a private home.

At the same time, there are practical limits to the refinements that can reasonably be introduced into Title III. A perfect system could conceivably differentiate between Internet and telephone communication, land-line and mobile phones, phones in residences and elsewhere, and—for some or all of these categories—investigations related to terrorism and investigations of other misconduct. But Title III is already an extraordinarily complex statute mandating highly elaborate safeguards and procedures. Law enforcement and individual privacy might both benefit from streamlining the Title III regime rather than introducing additional complications.

That concern suggests, at a minimum, that in this area policy-makers should not create separate authorities depending on the type of crime under investigation. Congress could consider excluding the least serious crimes from pen-register surveillance altogether, just as it has excluded them from the Title III wiretapping regime, but it does not make sense to subdivide further the existing offense categories. Similarly, it seems unwise to create a system giving higher levels of protection to some forms of pen-register monitoring than to others. Compared to telephone pen registers, Internet pen registers are more revealing in some ways but can be less revealing in others. (For one, Internet pen registers normally do not reveal whether a person is present in a particular location.) Telephones in homes probably deserve more protection than other phones but not to an extent that would justify the costs of maintaining separate statutory systems.

The principal decision therefore is whether to preserve the increasingly tenuous distinction between "addresses" and "content" or instead fold all pen-register and trap/trace monitoring into the stringent Title III regime that governs surveillance of substantive communication. The latter approach would greatly simplify the law and eliminate the pitfalls that confront investigators and courts attempting to determine whether an Internet pen register has intercepted "content." Unquestionably, however, that approach would prevent investigators from conducting some productive pen-register surveillance that was perfectly lawful before passage of the Patriot Act. Apart from obvious resistance to a move in that direction in the current political climate, the potential gains from simplification and more oversight do not seem concrete enough to justify the cost in terms of lost investigative information. (Among other benefits, pen-register surveillance is often a basis for determining whether to proceed with or block more intrusive surveillance of content.)

These considerations confirm the value of preserving separate regimes for pen-register monitoring and surveillance of content. At the same time, they underscore the importance of ensuring that pen registers be governed by safeguards commensurate with the significant concerns they raise and the "reasonable expectations of privacy" that clearly attach to the information affected. In this regard, the loose standards now applicable must be strengthened substantially.

First, there is a pressing need to clarify the line between "routing information" and "content." Unfortunately, in the context of Web browsing and Internet search terms this is much easier said than done, and in any event solutions that work today might not be viable or even relevant tomorrow. The Department of Justice has issued a memorandum instructing field offices to minimize the collection of content and to consult with headquarters to determine what constitutes content.[35] Such memorandums (redacted if necessary) and the standards used to make judgments about "content" should undoubtedly be made available for public comment and shared with the relevant congressional committees. The committees should, the sooner the better, explore possibilities for giving investigators and courts better guidance in the statute itself, and it should be possible to craft language making clear, for example, that search terms are to be treated as content.

Congress also should carry forward the existing provision of section 216 requiring investigators to file with the court a detailed log of all Internet pen-register and trap/trace surveillance, and it should extend that requirement to telephone pen-register and trap/trace devices as well. The danger of deliberate abuse or inadvertent collection of unauthorized material is much lower in the case of telephone monitoring (at least as conducted with today's technology), but maintenance of such logs is not difficult, and there is no reason to exempt telephone monitoring from after-the-fact reporting that the law properly requires for Internet monitoring and conventional wiretaps.

Congress should limit the use of pen-register and trap/trace devices to investigation of the same kinds of crimes that justify Title III wiretaps and electronic surveillance. This list has grown so inclusive that any significant federal investigation can easily meet the requirement. The change is nonetheless worth making to guarantee that intrusive pen-register surveillance of Internet usage and home telephones is not deployed in the investigation of minor federal misdemeanors. Even more important, section 216 currently allows a federal court to authorize pen-register and trap/trace surveillance at the behest of a *state* law enforcement officer investigating any criminal offense, no matter how trivial. Neither state nor federal officers should be able to obtain monitoring orders when investigating offenses not equivalent to those on the Title III list.

Finally, legislators can easily correct the most significant flaw in the current regime—the very loose factual predicate for trap/trace and pen-register surveillance. At present, for both telephone and Internet monitoring, the only requirement is that the information sought be "relevant to an ongoing criminal investigation." And the investigator's judgment about relevance is not subject to any independent judicial check. Those slender safeguards are fundamentally at odds with the particularity and independent screening that the constitution mandates for the kinds of intrusive surveillance that these devices permit.

Fourth Amendment law has already developed a well-understood standard of "specific and articulable facts" to meet the need in intermediate situations for a safeguard less demanding than probable cause but still sufficiently concrete and objective to permit meaningful judicial review.[36] This intermediate standard would enhance public trust and afford protection against the occasional "rogue" agent, but there is no reason to think it would pose a significant obstacle to legitimate pen-register and trap/trace monitoring. Indeed, one former Justice Department attorney with substantial experience in this area reports that, so far as he was aware, government agents seeking pen-register orders invariably had information sufficient to meet the more demanding "articulable facts" standard. Congress should amend the telephone and Internet provisions to require, as it has for other intermediate forms of electronic surveillance, that an application for pen-register or trap/trace authority must provide "specific and articulable facts showing reasonable grounds to believe that the information sought is relevant to an ongoing criminal investigation."[37]

SURVEILLANCE OF E-MAIL CONTENT ("CARNIVORE") (SECTION 216(B))

"Carnivore" is a software program developed by the FBI, which has since given it the less ominous name DCS 1000. Carnivore enables the FBI to enter the system of an Internet service provider (such as America Online) and record information passing through the ISP's network. It thus allows the FBI to monitor Internet and e-mail transmissions, including their content. Carnivore is designed to operate selectively, capturing only information that satisfies preset requirements, such as messages to or from a particular e-mail address. It can record all messages of a particular suspect, or it can be configured to record only selected content, a search that is potentially better targeted and less intrusive than a traditional wiretap. It can be used even more selectively as a pen-register or trap/trace device, picking up only a message's origin and destination identifiers. On the other hand, if not used in the most selective way, it can capture far more information than a conventional wiretap of a telephone.[38]

Only one provision of the Patriot Act deals with Carnivore. Section 216(b) requires that when a law enforcement agency uses its own programming system (such as Carnivore) as a pen-register or trap/trace device, the agency must keep and provide to the court a record of the information collected, the officers involved in collecting it, and the dates and times when the software was used.[39] The act in effect legitimates the use of Carnivore without probable cause, despite its ability to capture and record content, provided that it is configured to register only origin and destination identifiers. But, reflecting concerns about Carnivore's capacity for overbroad sweeps and other misuse, the act imposes reporting safeguards not required for conventional, less powerful pen-register and trap-trace technologies.

The use of Carnivore to capture the content of e-mail and Internet traffic is a search governed by the usual statutory restrictions (Title III and FISA).[40] The post–September 11 legislation confers no new authority for Carnivore searches, other than the expanded powers it confers for surveillance methods generally. But Carnivore searches will undoubtedly grow in significance as antiterrorism efforts and Internet usage expand.

Carnivore's potential for voraciously and indiscriminately devouring e-mail content makes it a potentially serious threat to the privacy of online communication. The Carnivore software may fail to filter out unrelated content, and, even if its filters work properly, agents who have access to it may deliberately or inadvertently misuse it. Perhaps of greatest concern is the "backdoor" problem. ISPs currently take great care to maintain the security of their networks, but Carnivore is designed to bypass all ISP security systems. This capability opens up a back door into the ISP's network, which could be exploited not only by a rogue agent but by any outsider able to hack into the FBI's Carnivore computers. An unauthorized user could spy on particular individuals or obtain their bank and credit card information without being detected by the ISP's security system.

An Illinois Institute of Technology (IIT) study team, in an independent technical review commissioned by the Department of Justice, concluded in December 2000 that many of the worst fears concerning Carnivore are unfounded.[41] It noted that Carnivore is a one-way system that can only receive and record; the software cannot alter information in the network, block network traffic, or shut down a Web site. Moreover, Carnivore, the report found, can function only when its filter is rather selective; it does not have enough power (at present) to spy on everyone or to record all e-mails flowing through an ISP network.

Nonetheless, Carnivore filters can malfunction. Although the IIT report found that properly configured Carnivore filters will work as intended, serious failures have occurred. In one of the worst, FBI agents conducting an e-mail surveillance of an al Qaeda target discovered in March 2000 that Carnivore had recorded not only the target's e-mail but that of many other network users. An FBI memo of April 5, 2000, reported that "the FBI technical person was apparently so upset that he destroyed all the e-mail take."[42]

The IIT study, moreover, reported other "significant deficiencies" in the Carnivore system. When used for pen-register and trap/trace purposes, it sometimes recorded more detail than authorized. It could be configured to perform sweeps far exceeding the permissible scope of a court-ordered search. FBI protocols did not sufficiently protect access to recorded information and physical access to Carnivore computers. Most important, the system's structure made it impossible to identify the individual agents using Carnivore, so that supervisors could not determine which agent did what in connection with its operation. As a result, the study team "did not find adequate provisions (for example, audit trails) for establishing individual accountability for actions taken during use of Carnivore."[43]

To date, more than four years after the IIT report was completed, the FBI has given no public indication that these deficiencies have been corrected. Until they are, Carnivore will pose a troubling and increasing threat to the privacy of Internet communication.[44]

COMPUTER TRESPASSERS (SECTION 217)

Prior to the Patriot Act, wiretapping and e-mail content surveillance normally required a warrant issued on probable cause. But the statutes contained two important exceptions authorizing limited forms of surveillance without a warrant. One allowed any party to the communication to record it or to grant the government permission to record it. The other allowed the provider of a communications service to monitor any transmissions through its network when necessary for "the protection of the rights or property of the provider of that service."[45] In the latter case, the surveillance would expose the communication to someone who was *not* an intended party to it. The need for that breach of privacy arose when individuals found a way to tap into the telephone system and make unlimited long-distance calls without being charged for them. The provider exception allows the phone company to conduct surveillance for the limited purpose of ensuring that the use of its network is reserved for legitimate subscribers. This right of surveillance, however, is limited to the system owner itself; the service provider cannot authorize government participation in the monitoring.

The same two exceptions apply to e-mail surveillance. The first is much less significant, of course, because recording of e-mail communications is automatic in any event. But the provider exception remains important to enable an Internet service provider (ISP) to make sure that those using its network are in fact authorized to do so. If anything, the provider exception has become increasingly important as computer hacking grows more prevalent and more damaging.

Unfortunately, the technicalities of Internet surveillance law created great uncertainty about whether the provider and consent exceptions could in fact be invoked where they were most needed—to intercept and trace computer hackers. Typically, a hacker, to avoid detection, will route his attack through a long, circuitous chain of computer servers before directing it to its intended target. In this situation, the owner of the target computer—the victim of the attack—is presumably a party to the communication and can consent to monitoring by government investigators. The investigators, in turn, can quickly trace the attack back to the immediately preceding server.

At that step, however, the legal technicalities create a large pitfall. None of the available doctrines quite fits the circumstances. The provider exception is presumably available to the owner of that intermediate server, but a provider cannot delegate its monitoring privilege to the government. The owner of the intermediate server can monitor the transmission to protect its own rights, but pursuit of the hacker will stall unless that owner has the willingness and expertise to join the chase. Conversely, the consent exception does allow delegation of monitoring rights to the government, but this exception can be invoked only by a "party to the communication."

The problem, then, is to determine whether an intermediate computer in the chain is a party to the communication. Were the courts willing to say that it is, they could solve the computer hacker problem quickly, but that solution would gut the system of statutory safeguards for e-mail: if an intermediate ISP were a "party" to e-mail passing through its server, then it would have the right to read all that e-mail, in clear violation of the privacy that the surveillance statutes were meant to protect. If, however, the intermediate ISP is not considered a "party," then it cannot enlist government help in tracing the hacker, and many investigations will be thwarted for technical reasons having nothing to do with legitimate privacy rights. The net effect of the law, as it stood before the Patriot Act, was somewhat similar to having a rule that barred government surveillance of a burglar, even at the invitation of a property owner whose land was being used as a path to the burglar's intended target.

One should note, of course, that the complexities under discussion, however important, do not pose a significant obstacle to fighting terrorism. Computer hacking, if used as a means to wreak havoc on the computer systems of the Defense Department, an airline, or a major bank, could indeed become a terrorist tactic. But this was not the central concern of the Justice Department's computer crime specialists either before or after September 11. The dilemma posed by the technicalities of the provider and consent exceptions had little to do with terrorism. It was nonetheless a genuine problem calling for a statutory fix.

Section 217 of the Patriot Act tackled the problem by authorizing government investigators, at the invitation of the victim of a computer attack, to monitor communications of an unauthorized user to, from, or through a protected computer. The owner of the computer in question must authorize the surveillance on its system, and investigators must have reasonable grounds to believe that the communications to be intercepted will be relevant to their investigation. Furthermore, the monitoring must cease at the conclusion of the investigation.

Section 217 also includes two important safeguards that limit the scope of the computer-trespasser exception. First, it makes clear that the exception does not extend to all unauthorized users of an ISP but only to trespassers who have no contractual relationship with the ISP at all. Thus, if a subscriber is using his or her computer in an unauthorized way—illegally downloading music, for example—the computer-trespasser exception would not apply, and surveillance would be permissible only if authorized by a warrant. Second, government investigators can invoke the trespasser exception only if the computer system's software allows them to intercept only the communications of the trespasser himself; the exception does not apply (and thus, warrantless monitoring would not be allowed) if the system's configuration could lead to interception of communications of authorized users.

Nonetheless, some privacy advocates have criticized the trespasser exception as excessively broad because it does not call for any judicial oversight and makes no provision for notifying law-abiding users whose e-mail was inadvertently or mistakenly intercepted.[46] The same problems, however, arise throughout law enforcement: an individual's voluntary consent is always sufficient to authorize police search or surveillance of his or her property, without judicial oversight and without any after-the-fact notification of parties who may have been observed or overheard. The risks of abuse are no doubt somewhat greater in the absence of these safeguards, but the requirement of independent citizen consent provides a check on law enforcement overreaching. Overall, the dangers in this narrow area seem limited.

Section 217 is scheduled to sunset in December 2005. It cannot plausibly be defended as a counterterrorism measure. But it is, on the whole, a justified and largely well targeted tool of general law enforcement. Though it is worth a close reexamination, section 217 is a useful measure that deserves to be carried forward.

SHARING OF GRAND JURY INFORMATION (SECTIONS 203(A) & (C))

Civil liberties discussions typically focus on the threshold rules that limit government access to private information. But other rules of great practical importance limit the use and dissemination *within* government of private information that some agency does have a right to acquire.

Prior to September 11, the Federal Rules of Criminal Procedure prohibited prosecutors from disclosing any "matter occurring before the grand jury."[47] As a result, they normally could not reveal important intelligence they had garnered from grand jury witnesses, even to other federal officials who might have legitimate needs for it. A few exceptions allowed disclosure for federal law enforcement purposes and for certain other restricted purposes when specifically authorized by the court supervising the grand jury. But the exceptions were tightly policed by the courts, and they were not broad enough to permit routine disclosure to CIA analysts or FBI foreign intelligence investigators.

These stringent guarantees of secrecy were thought necessary for a number of reasons: to prevent flight by suspects under investigation, to insulate grand jurors from improper influence, to keep suspects from intimidating potential witnesses, to encourage witnesses to give candid and complete testimony, and to protect suspects under investigation from damage to their reputations.[48] Nonetheless, the secrecy rules had the effect of impeding coordination and erecting another "wall" between different components of the law enforcement and intelligence communities.

Section 203(a) of the Patriot Act resolved that problem by authorizing prosecutors to disclose to appropriate national security and counterterrorism officials, for use in their official duties, any grand jury material that involves "foreign intelligence or counterintelligence information."[49] As a partial safeguard, section 203(a) requires that when grand jury information is disclosed under the new provision, the prosecutor must promptly file with the court a notice indicating the information disclosed and the agency to which it was given.[50] In addition, section 203(c) directs the attorney general to establish procedures regulating such disclosures, presumably to limit the risks of abuse. By July 2002 the Department of Justice reported that it had already made extensive use of the section 203 powers; disclosure of foreign intelligence information obtained through grand juries had been made on approximately forty occasions, involving investigations in thirty-eight districts.[51]

Unlike many of the Patriot Act's law enforcement reforms, the grand jury amendment is narrowly tailored—information unrelated to foreign intelligence and counterterrorism remains subject to the prior restrictions. On the other hand, this amendment was exempted from the act's sunset provisions, and critics fear that the new authority, even with its focus on terrorism, will prove too dangerous, tempting investigators to exploit the grand jury's exceptionally strong powers and to misuse properly acquired information. During the brief congressional debates that preceded passage of the Patriot Act, Senator Patrick Leahy singled out the new authority to disseminate grand jury information as a particular "invitation to abuse"[52] and expressed concern that this power could permit a recreation of the FBI misconduct documented by the Church Committee in the 1970s (see Chapter 2).

THE NEED

How serious a problem was the confidentiality rule that governed grand juries before the Patriot Act? Some have drawn a nearly direct line between the old secrecy rules and the failure to foil the September 11 plot. Less than a month after the attacks, Stewart Baker, a former general counsel of the National Security Agency, wrote in the *Wall Street Journal* that "grand jury secrecy rules may be one reason we didn't anticipate" September 11: "Whoever dreamed up the first World Trade Center bombing was probably also behind the second attack. Who conceived and organized that first attack? We can't be sure, in part because the CIA was hobbled in its review of the first attack—by grand jury secrecy."[53]

Details that have since come to light, however, make clear that the grand jury rules were not in any way to blame. The proceedings in the first World Trade Center bombing case, brought in 1996, did contain a wealth of valuable information, but much of the telling detail became part of the trial record, and it was readily available to the CIA (and, indeed, to the general public) long before the second attack.[54] Conversely, there were no telltale clues lurking unexamined in the grand jury records.[55] The problem, as all subsequent inquiries have concluded, was the analysts' failure to appreciate the significance of the information available to them.[56]

Nonetheless, it is easy to imagine ways in which the restrictive rules could interfere with effective coordination and analysis. In fact, a U.S. attorney who had worked on counterterrorism matters in the 1990s testified about one instance in which the compartmentalization of grand jury intelligence nearly led investigators to make the wrong decision about whether to arrest a suspect in the 1998 embassy bombings case. The misstep was narrowly averted in that instance, but, as the prosecutor recalled, "The team got lucky, but we never should have had to rely on luck. . . . [T]he 'wall' could easily have caused a different decision . . . that would have allowed a key player in the al Qaeda network to escape. . . ."[57]

Thus, there is little doubt that steps toward greater flexibility in handling grand jury information are warranted in the aftermath of September 11. Critics largely accept that conclusion but focus on the need to secure adequate oversight of the ways in which this flexibility is used.[58]

Adequate Oversight

The initial House version of the Patriot Act allowed disclosure of grand jury information only with prior court approval, but the Senate version mandated no prior or subsequent judicial notification at all.[59] The final language, a compromise, required only *subsequent* notification.[60] In September 2002 the attorney general, pursuant to section 203(c), issued privacy guidelines specifying that grand jury information disseminated within the government must be labeled to identify the applicable secrecy restrictions and must be handled according to protocols designed to ensure appropriate use.[61]

Many grand jury experts consider these measures insufficient. Several would restore in some form the stronger judicial oversight mechanism envisaged by the House bill.[62] Two critics urge prior approval by the court supervising the grand jury as the only means "to keep the grand jury's investigation within proper bounds."[63] One former federal prosecutor suggests that local judges would have insufficient expertise and an excessive tendency to defer to the government in national security matters. She proposes instead a requirement of prior authorization by a specially designated group of judges, modeled on the Foreign Intelligence Surveillance Court, along with an obligation for the prosecutor to provide "the precise identities of the individuals receiving grand jury information" and to certify that recipients have been informed of the secrecy restrictions attached to the information.[64]

A prior-authorization requirement of this nature would provide a reassuring safeguard against abuse. But the added "red tape" might in practice recreate a "wall" or at least a significant deterrent to sharing information quickly, when it can be most useful. Of course, prior approval could be waived in exigent circumstances. But since the new sharing provisions apply only to foreign intelligence information—information that often, if not inevitably, will be time sensitive—the burden of separating the truly urgent situations from the others and then obtaining prior authorization only for the latter may not be worth the trouble.

It must be remembered that threshold privacy rights are not at issue here. No matter how sensitive, the information has already been revealed to the government. It is only the degree of dissemination that is at stake, and scrutiny by the courts, though important, is inevitably needed less than in situations when the power to intrude is asserted. On balance, a requirement of prior judicial authorization seems likely to prove more cumbersome than the circumstances warrant.

A more workable alternative would be to introduce a mechanism for a formal congressional check. Indeed, the lack of strong judicial control in these circumstances underscores the importance of accountability through the congressional oversight process. And the burden of a detailed, after-the-fact reporting requirement would be minimal because the statute already requires prosecutors to file notification with the court every time that a foreign intelligence dissemination is made. The Justice Department should be obligated to file comprehensive statistics on these disclosures with the Judiciary or Intelligence Committees, and, as needed, prosecutors should be responsible for making available redacted records indicating the substance of the information disclosed and the identity of the agencies or individual officials who received it.[65] Congressional oversight of this sort poses little to no risk of impeding genuine counterterrorism operations, but it would greatly diminish the dangers presented by the broad disclosure powers of section 203.

TECHNICAL CHANGES AND ROUTINE CORRECTIONS

Several of the Patriot Act's new search and surveillance provisions merely correct technical oversights and anomalies in prior law. For example, through a quirk in statutory wording, government could use a search warrant to obtain records of unopened e-mail but not records of unopened messages stored in a voice mail system. Similarly, the law permitted the use of search warrants to obtain communication records from telephone and Internet access companies but not from cable companies that provide identical services. Eleven sections of the act adjust these and similar anomalies. Because these provisions confer surveillance authority that did not exist before September 11, 2001, they can be criticized as inappropriately expanding government power. But, as explained below, none of these measures grants powers significantly different from those authorized long before September 11. Although seven of the eleven provisions are scheduled to sunset, none intrudes on privacy in any new way, and none should be considered controversial.

TITLE III SURVEILLANCE IN TERRORISM CASES (SECTION 201)

Under the Fourth Amendment, wiretapping and electronic surveillance must be authorized through a search warrant supported by probable cause. In addition, Title III imposes additional requirements designed to restrict this intrusive form of surveillance to situations of strong investigative need. For example, the crime under investigation must be one designated in Title III as particularly serious. Murder, espionage, racketeering, and extortion are obvious examples. But Title III's list of designated offenses has expanded over time to include such less serious crimes as bribery, money laundering, theft from interstate shipment, embezzlement from a pension fund, gambling, and obscenity.

Section 201 adds terrorism offenses to the list of crimes considered serious enough to justify electronic eavesdropping when probable cause exists. Who could disagree? Some might worry that the concept of terrorism could be stretched to cover activities that should be sheltered from intensive government surveillance—political protest and low-level civil disobedience, to name two. But here the Patriot Act was careful enough to define the terrorism offenses specifically and to limit them to situations involving intentional killing and other extremely dangerous misconduct. Because even before the Patriot Act, the law authorized electronic surveillance to investigate gambling enterprises, theft, and extortion, there is ample reason to confer the same power where terrorism is concerned. Indeed, section 201 seems to present a vivid example of the compelling need for the Patriot Act to correct absurd statutory gaps. The absence of terrorism offenses from the Title III list of serious crimes seems an inexcusable restriction on law enforcement.

One might wonder why terrorism was excluded from the Title III list before September 11. In fact, it was not. Any act sufficiently heinous to fit the definition of terrorism would almost inevitably come under the heading of murder, extortion, or some other offense already included in the Title III list. Under prior law, there was no significant gap to fill. By the same token, section 201 creates no new government power and no fresh risk of abuse. Although section 201 is due to sunset, its effects are purely technical, and it should not be controversial in any way.

TITLE III SURVEILLANCE IN COMPUTER FRAUD CASES (SECTION 202)

Unlike section 201, section 202 seems to have little if anything to do with the September 11 attacks or with terrorism in general. It adds another offense to the list of crimes that can be investigated through Title III surveillance, namely, felony computer fraud or abuse.

In this instance there is plenty of room to argue that the offense is not serious enough to warrant intrusive surveillance. Of course, computers can be used to plan a serious terror attack, but investigators in such a case could justify Title III surveillance on many other grounds (attempted murder, extortion, or terrorism) without having to claim "computer fraud or abuse." Even if the terrorists' target were not buildings or people but only a computer system itself, their plot would almost certainly qualify as extortion, malicious mischief, or interference with commerce by threats, all offenses already eligible for investigation under Title III.

What section 202 adds, therefore, is not a new tool to fight terrorism but rather a weapon to fight computer fraud in general, even when it is not related to the terror threat. By folding this provision into the Patriot Act, at a time when Congress and the public were preoccupied with terrorism, the Department of Justice left itself open to charges of opportunism and exploitation of September 11 to pursue unrelated goals. Those understandable perceptions have done much to discredit the Patriot Act as a whole.

That said, section 202 can now be reassessed simply as a tool to aid general law enforcement. From that perspective, the case for it is reasonably strong. Title III already authorizes electronic surveillance to investigate mail fraud, telemarketing abuse ("wire fraud"), and other commercial frauds. Absent section 202, a fraudulent solicitation arguably would be sheltered from a Title III investigation in some situations simply because it was perpetrated by e-mail rather than by mail or telephone—surely an arbitrary distinction. Eliminating that anomaly is a technical matter, and although section 202 is slated to sunset, its renewal should not be considered controversial.

SHARING OF FOREIGN INTELLIGENCE INFORMATION (SECTIONS 203(B) & (D))

Just as section 203(a) authorizes prosecutors to disseminate foreign intelligence information obtained through a grand jury investigation, section 203(b) authorizes law enforcement agents to disclose to national security and counterterrorism officials any foreign intelligence information that is the fruit of a Title III surveillance. Section 203(d) authorizes law enforcement agents to disclose on a similar basis any foreign intelligence information gathered in other ways during the course of a criminal investigation. Both of these provisions are scheduled to sunset, but they concern an area that is less sensitive and subject to far fewer restrictions than those traditionally applicable to grand jury material. The need for flexibility in regard to this sort of information sharing is reasonably clear, and formal requirements of judicial or congressional oversight seem more burdensome that the circumstances call for. On balance, the renewal of these provisions should not be considered controversial.

Seizure of Voice Mail (Section 209)

Before September 11 investigators were allowed to use a conventional search warrant to obtain records of unopened e-mail and to obtain access to messages recorded on a home answering machine. But they needed to follow a much more complex procedure and meet more demanding standards—those of a Title III wiretap order—when they sought records of unopened messages in a voice mail system.

The more demanding standard makes sense when investigators cast the relatively wide and indiscriminate net involved in attempts to intercept ongoing communications in "real time." But that standard is less appropriate when investigators merely seek access to stored messages left by or for a particular suspect, and the law reflects that judgment in allowing the use of a conventional search warrant for obtaining stored e-mail and answering machine messages. There is no significant reason for different treatment of messages stored in a voice mail system.

Indeed, as information technology has evolved, the distinction between e-mail and oral messages is beginning to collapse. Through use of systems such as MIME (Multipurpose Internet Mail Extensions), voice recordings can now be sent as attachments to e-mail. If different procedures applied to these two forms of communication, as they did under pre–September 11 law, investigations involving unopened e-mail would raise daunting legal complexities. Investigators would use an ordinary search warrant to obtain access to that e-mail, but if they discovered an attachment, they would need to determine whether the message on it was in oral or written form before they could legally open it. And if they discovered that the attachment was oral, they would need to obtain a new surveillance order under the more demanding wiretap standard before they could learn its content.

An obstacle course of this sort would serve no purpose, and section 209 properly eliminated it by allowing the use of conventional search warrants for both unopened e-mail and stored voice messages. This provision, which sunsets, applies not only to terrorism investigations but also in situations involving routine criminal offenses. The Justice Department acknowledges that it has been used to investigate "a variety of criminal cases."[66] Nonetheless, as a tool of ordinary law enforcement, section 209 is well justified, and it should be renewed as noncontroversial.

SUBPOENAS FOR COMMUNICATIONS CUSTOMER RECORDS (SECTION 210)

Prior to the Patriot Act, the law authorized the use of subpoenas to obtain certain records pertaining to telephone company customers, such as the customer's name, address, and means of payment. But the authorized disclosures did not extend to credit card numbers or other details that might be necessary to establish the customer's true identity, and that gap has become more significant with the wider use of cell phones, e-mail, and other forms of communication not tied to a fixed location. In addition, the law applicable to these subpoenas prior to 2001 authorized disclosure of information specific to telephone calls (the billing records showing the time of day and duration of local and long-distance calls), but its language did not cover the analogous time-of-day and duration details for e-mail communications.

Section 210 filled these gaps by expanding the list of records that investigators can obtain by subpoena. As amended, the law now extends to the customer's means and source of payment (including the account number of the credit card or bank account used) and to the "session times and duration" of communications, whether by telephone, e-mail, or other forms of transmission. Although the provision permits government to ascertain specific facts that were not so readily accessible prior to September 11, the information covered is not significantly more private than the parallel types of information already obtainable from older communications technologies.

Section 210 is not limited to terrorism investigations, and in fact its primary importance is in the investigation of crimes committed online, including child pornography and computer hacking. It has been used to help trace suspects in a range of cases, including one in which computer hackers had targeted more than fifty government and military computers.[67] Section 210 does not sunset, and, because it produces little substantive change in the reach of the subpoena power, a close reexamination is unnecessary.

SEARCH WARRANTS FOR CABLE COMPANY RECORDS (SECTION 211)

Before September 11 the law permitted the use of subpoenas and search warrants to obtain communication records from telephone and Internet access companies, but it required a more cumbersome procedure, with notice to the customer and a full adversary hearing, to obtain records from cable companies. The more rigorous procedures and stronger safeguards were justified because of the more personal nature of cable programming services. A cable customer's choices lie much closer to protected freedoms of speech and the press, and the associated records typically reveal information that is considered more private, such as the specific channels a particular customer watches.

With changes in technology, however, many cable companies now provide telephone and Internet services as well. If cable companies, phone companies, and ISPs are offering identical services, there is no good reason to impose more stringent standards for one type of provider than for the others. And the elaborate safeguards of a full adversary hearing are inappropriate (not to mention fatal to clandestine surveillance) when the records sought pertain only to routine communications.

Section 211 handles this problem by subjecting cable companies to the same, relatively streamlined subpoena and search warrant process that governs phone companies and ISPs. The change, however, does not apply in the case of cable company records pertaining to "customer cable television viewing activity," thus preserving distinct treatment where the stricter safeguards remain justified. Section 211 was drafted with some care. It does not sunset, and it need not be reconsidered.

EMERGENCY DISCLOSURES (SECTION 212)

As a result of several quirks in statutory wording, the law used to prohibit communications service providers from disclosing private customer information (such as records of calls or the content of e-mails), even in an emergency such as the threat of an imminent attack, where prompt disclosure to law enforcement could save lives. Section 212 corrects this oversight by authorizing voluntary disclosure by the service provider in emergencies "involving immediate danger of death or serious physical injury to any person."

Although the emergency disclosure provision could conceivably help disrupt a major international terrorist plot, its primary applications will more likely arise in conventional law enforcement situations. The Justice Department reports, for example, that section 212 has been used to prevent the success of a bomb threat against a high school and a threat to kill company executives as part of an attempt to extort a ransom. In both instances, it was instrumental in enabling investigators to identify and arrest the perpetrators.[68]

Section 212 should not be considered controversial, and, although scheduled to sunset, it deserves to be renewed.

NATIONWIDE SEARCH WARRANTS (SECTIONS 216(C), 219, AND 220)

Under the law before September 11, a search warrant and most other surveillance orders were valid only within the federal district where they were issued. As a result, prosecutors were required to file a separate search warrant application in each district where a search or surveillance might occur. This process was especially cumbersome for electronic surveillance of e-mail and Internet traffic. Internet service providers are often located far from the center of an investigation, and many ISPs are concentrated in locations such as Silicon Valley, California, where judges and magistrates were faced with large numbers of applications unrelated to any local criminal activity. In addition, a computer hacking attack typically proceeds through a large number of servers, and investigators often identify the first ones only after surveillance of a server that followed them in the chain. A hacking investigation could therefore necessitate many separate surveillance orders; it would require the participation of prosecutors and magistrates based in many federal districts, and most of the officials drawn into the application process would have no real involvement in the investigation.

Several sections of the Patriot Act attempt to streamline this process by authorizing federal judges and magistrates to issue orders effective nationwide under certain circumstances. Section 216(c) gives nationwide reach to pen-register and trap/trace orders; section 219 permits certain conventional search and arrest warrants to be enforced across the country; and section 220 is applicable nationwide to orders for the recovery of stored e-mail. In each case the order must be for the investigation of an offense committed at least in part in the district where the issuing court sits, but when this condition is met, the order is valid anywhere in the United States.

Although the rationale for these changes is similar in all three cases, different limitations are imposed in each. For persons and tangible property, the authority to issue nationwide search and arrest warrants is limited to investigations of domestic or international terrorism; this provision does not sunset. For stored e-mail, the powers are not limited to terrorism investigations, but this provision does sunset. And the nationwide pen-register and trap/trace authority is neither limited to terrorism cases nor subject to sunset; in fact, both of the latter provisions have been used frequently to investigate a variety of offenses unrelated to terrorism, including theft and the flight of a fugitive.[69]

Though the convenience for investigators of a nationwide warrant is easy to appreciate, the need is much less pressing in the case of ordinary physical searches, which do not involve the unique difficulties of surveillance orders directed to ISPs. On the other hand, even in the case of physical searches, geographical limitations can delay the application process. In instances where such delays can be most problematic, it seems wise to streamline the process. The important point with respect to these search and arrest warrants is that regardless of where the warrant may be served, it can be issued in the first place only after independent judicial review that establishes probable cause on the basis of objective circumstances. Once that requirement is met, the geographical reach of the warrant poses relatively little additional risk to the privacy interests involved.

In that light, section 219 strikes a reasonable balance, permitting a nationwide writ for physical search and arrest warrants in terrorism investigations (where delays can be especially costly) but preserving the usual geographical limitations in investigations of common crime. Section 219 does not sunset, and it seems worth preserving in its present form.

Regarding orders for pen registers, trap/trace devices, and the recovery of stored e-mail, the considerations are more complex.

Geographical limitations can pose a much more serious obstacle for investigators. The difficulties are not limited to terrorism inquiries; they can be especially frustrating, for example, in computer hacking cases. But orders with a nationwide reach can be problematic for ISPs that are their targets. If they wish to challenge the order or ask the court to clarify its scope, they may be obliged to begin legal proceedings in a court that could be anywhere in the country.[70] The burden could be especially great for smaller ISPs. Because the scope of these kinds of surveillance orders is often ill defined, it seems essential to provide some mechanism for promptly and conveniently clarifying them.

For the relatively infrequent situations in which judicial clarification may be sought, it should be feasible to permit the ISP facing the order to present its challenge in the federal district where it is located. To be sure, multidistrict involvement by prosecutors would then become necessary, recreating in part the burdens the Justice Department had to contend with before passage of the Patriot Act. But such situations would be exceptional, rather than inevitable (and typically pointless), as they were before the Patriot Act. Subject to the need to provide a local forum for resolving ISP challenges, both of the amendments relating to electronic surveillance orders—sections 216(c) and 220—seem reasonably well justified. Although the latter provision sunsets, while the former does not, both sections are worth keeping in roughly their present form.

Chapter 6

SECURITY AND FREEDOM FOR THE LONG HAUL

In its efforts to identify, track, disrupt, and prevent terrorist activity, the government has a genuine need for surveillance tools different from those it deploys in ordinary domestic law enforcement. There are legitimate reasons for heightened secrecy and modified systems of accountability.

Yet neither "foreign intelligence" nor even "war" are talismans that suspend accountability or the Fourth Amendment altogether. They have not done so in past American wars, and they have not done so in other Western democracies that have struggled over many decades against unremitting terrorist threats.[1] Despite the heightened importance of agility, secrecy, and speed in counterterrorism matters, it also is vital to preserve strong accountability mechanisms and the essence of constitutional checks and balances. We must do so to safeguard privacy, to prevent overreaching, and to ensure effectiveness in the counterterrorism effort itself. As a result, Americans must not suspend civil liberties safeguards to a greater degree than necessary. And when it is truly necessary to do so, law makers must craft substitute safeguards that will preserve the essence of accountability and protect the rule of law from the dangers of unchecked executive power.

The Patriot Act has many virtues, and they are acknowledged in detail throughout this report. Nonetheless, the statute remains gravely flawed. It gives almost no weight to the *hidden costs* of a powerfully expanded intelligence-gathering capability. It fails to draw *reasonable boundaries;* as a result, it permits unnecessary intrusions on privacy and dangerous incursions on First Amendment freedoms of speech, press, and religion. Even where federal powers are justifiably enlarged, the legislation fails to guarantee appropriate *accountability.* Case-by-case judicial scrutiny, after-the-fact remedies, and congressional oversight all must be strengthened— and easily can be—without impeding the continuing, uphill struggle to establish a smoothly run and effective intelligence-gathering effort.

THE HIDDEN COSTS

One of the most serious concerns raised by laws like the Patriot Act, as serious as the threat they pose to civil liberties, is the risk that they will divert attention and energy from solving problems that are far more serious. With or without the Patriot Act, counterterrorism efforts will continue to face major obstacles that have nothing to do with legal requirements or the preservation of civil liberties.

The list of the most important national security deficits is depressingly long, but it is nonetheless essential to spell them out in order to keep some perspective on the "liberty versus security" debate that so often dominates public discussion. Any catalog of the weaknesses that remain acute more than three years after September 11, 2001, must include:

- ◆ insufficient resources and planning for the protection of critical infrastructure, especially ports, weapons facilities, and chemical plants, any one of which, if attacked, could cause hundreds of thousands of deaths or billions of dollars in economic damage;

- ◆ ongoing difficulty in setting up and coordinating the sprawling new Department of Homeland Security;

- ◆ continued problems of organization and communication within and between the FBI, the CIA, and the other frontline agencies of law enforcement and intelligence, most of which remain outside the already vast DHS bureaucracy;

◆   scarcity of competent translators in languages such as Arabic, Urdu, and Farsi;

◆   severe shortages of personnel and resources generally; and

◆   failure to modernize the FBI computer system, which continues to impair communication among agents and their capabilities to search the FBI's own internal database.

To be sure, the persistence of these structural difficulties should not stop us from addressing legal issues—particularly when legal problems can be fixed without putting important liberties at risk. But with so many obstacles standing in the way of the capacity to digest, analyze, disseminate, and use the intelligence acquired, it would be foolish to think that laws permitting a wider intelligence-gathering net will automatically make the country safer. Until the fundamental problems of personnel, resources, and organization are solved, the benefits of expanded intelligence-gathering powers will be far less than most Americans imagine. The overriding priority therefore must be to fix the huge nonlegal deficiencies that currently hamper efforts to gather and use information effectively.

Stronger intelligence-gathering authority entails other large costs. The losses of privacy and the potential intrusions on freedoms of speech and religion are obvious but important to reemphasize. An especially important instance is the unprecedented and alarming new FISA power authorizing the FBI to cull library, bookstore, and religious affiliation records of citizens not in any way suspected of wrongdoing. Acceptance of broad powers like this one will chill dissent and religious freedom, work gradual but important long-term changes on America's culture of political liberty, and permanently erode the foundations of American democracy.

Beyond these large but relatively familiar dangers is the more complex risk that information acquired for legitimate reasons will be misused. There is no need to speculate about potential harms, because our own recent history provides far too many concrete examples. Now as in the past, the overwhelming majority of FBI agents are conscientious professionals. Yet, prior to the intelligence reforms of the 1970s, broad FBI surveillance powers were extensively exploited for illegitimate purposes. As the Church Committee found in the mid-1970s, the FBI's intelligence collection programs "generate[d] ever-increasing demands for new data"[2] and quickly produced more than half a million domestic intelligence files, many of them focused on legitimate protest organizations, on both the left and the right, that were considered radical or extremist in their time.[3]

Perhaps surprisingly, overly broad intelligence-gathering powers undermine effective law enforcement. Absent the discipline that results from requiring objective justification at the outset and independent oversight after the fact, many of the new Patriot Act surveillance powers will inevitably produce "mission creep," wasting limited resources and misdirecting agents' time and effort. Lacking a mandate for selectivity in the choice of surveillance techniques and targets, energetic investigators deploying their new Patriot Act powers can quickly overload the intelligence process, swamping translators and analysts, clogging the channels of information, and impeding the flow of genuinely useful intelligence.

Most important, the new Patriot Act powers impair the perceived legitimacy of the entire law enforcement enterprise. To make progress in combating terrorism requires gaining the trust of Muslim Americans, immigrants, and other minority communities in the United States as well as similar communities around the world. To do so, it is not enough to assume that others will take America's good intentions for granted. Our government must make clear its commitment to using its great power with restraint and with respect for the rule of law, both abroad and here at home. Without that trust, strong surveillance powers will quickly become self-defeating. It is essential, therefore, that surveillance powers be subject to reasonable boundaries, and that appropriate accountability mechanisms be in place to guarantee that the boundaries are effective. Yet, in too many important respects, the Patriot Act fails to satisfy these imperatives.

REASONABLE BOUNDARIES

An extraordinary threat properly calls forth extraordinary powers, but their hidden costs make it essential that these powers be narrowly tailored. Otherwise, their application can easily backfire, undermining *both* liberty and security. Yet, the Patriot Act is pervaded with provisions that respond to legitimate needs by granting powers much broader than necessary. For example:

♦ The act rightly dismantles the FISA wall and makes FISA available even when foreign intelligence objectives are not an investigator's exclusive concern. But with that barrier out of the way, it leaves little restriction on prosecutors' ability to use special FISA powers in conventional law enforcement.

♦ The Patriot Act properly extends pen-register surveillance—the technique of tracking the origin and destination of a communication—from telephone transmissions to e-mail. This type of surveillance can be regulated less tightly than wiretapping because pen-register surveillance is supposed to leave inviolate the privacy of the communication's content. Those considerations do not, however, mean that such surveillance should be left essentially unregulated. Yet, the Patriot Act does not require investigators using a pen register to have any objective basis for their suspicions, and it does not limit the use of pen registers to terrorism investigations or even to felony investigations of any sort. Pen-register surveillance requires nothing more than a hunch concerning the possible commission of a minor offense.

♦ The Patriot Act also takes insufficient steps to match theory and reality by preventing pen-register surveillance from being used to acquire the content of e-mail and Internet transmissions, such as the search terms that an individual uses when surfing the Web.

♦ The Patriot Act justifiably endorses the use of delayed notice (sneak-and-peek) searches in domestic law enforcement. But it imposes only vague limits on the circumstances needed to authorize a sneak and peek and on the length of time that notice can be delayed.

♦ The Patriot Act allows for secret searches in foreign intelligence investigations and legitimately regulates them more loosely than the secret sneak-and-peek searches of domestic law enforcement. Yet, it leaves secret FISA searches unconstrained by conventional safeguards that would not in any way impede counterespionage and counterterrorism efforts. Prosecutors involved in ordinary domestic law enforcement can initiate and control these highly intrusive searches; they do not have to demonstrate any need in order to keep the search hidden from the affected homeowner; and the permanent secrecy of the search is automatic, again, regardless of need.

- ◆ The Patriot Act expands, for good reason, the kinds of documents that the FBI can obtain from third parties without showing probable cause. But it frees the FBI from providing any justification for its document demands and imposes no limits at all on the kinds of records that can be obtained in this way. Records of the most sensitive nature—medical histories, library transactions, and religious membership lists—are all exposed to scrutiny on the same relatively unregulated basis as the most banal telephone and electric bills.

Indiscriminate powers like these not only sacrifice liberty needlessly but actually *impede* bona fide law enforcement efforts.

MAXIMUM FEASIBLE ACCOUNTABILITY

The unique challenges of the struggle against terrorism make maximum feasible accountability especially important. The Patriot Act, however, is full of provisions that needlessly restrict or eliminate executive branch accountability for its actions. Many provisions are structured to minimize the occasions for effective judicial review and to make sure that useful information about the use of extraordinary powers will be placed beyond the reach of public and congressional scrutiny. For example:

- ◆ The Department of Justice need not publish any information about its use of the sneak and peek, even with respect to the use of such searches in ordinary domestic law enforcement.

- ◆ Congressional oversight committees have little access to the most general information, even aggregate statistics, concerning the government's use of special foreign intelligence surveillance tools.

◆ A law-abiding citizen targeted for a clandestine FISA physical search is never notified that his or her home was invaded and thus is never afforded the opportunity to challenge the legality of the intrusion. Civil remedies for other misconduct in a foreign intelligence investigation are virtually meaningless because innocent individuals cannot learn whether they were subjected to FISA electronic surveillance, even long after the fact.

◆ An organization instructed to produce documents about its members or contributors faces an automatic and indefinite gag order that prevents it from ever bringing overbroad or abusive orders to the attention of the press. Likewise, the organization is forever barred from notifying the person whose records were affected.

◆ Defense counsel who seek to suppress the results of an allegedly illegal FISA surveillance are afforded little direct access to the information necessary to mount an effective challenge.

◆ Judges are required to issue a document production order whenever the FBI asks them to do so. The courts have no authority to review the need for the order or the existence of any objective basis for it.

These are shortcomings that can easily be fixed. Doing so will make our liberties more secure and our counterterrorism efforts more rather than less effective.

RECOMMENDATIONS

Many Patriot Act provisions scheduled to sunset deserve to be reenacted. However, four groups of investigative powers require significant revision—those relating to pen-register devices, secret physical searches, foreign intelligence surveillance, and document production orders. In these areas, lawmakers must act to rein in powers that threaten core liberties and pose substantial dangers of abuse. Cutting across all these distinct powers, moreover, is the need for much stronger oversight structures within the executive branch and in Congress.

UNNECESSARY SUNSETS

Of the Patriot Act provisions scheduled to sunset on December 31, 2005, ten are reasonable measures that should be renewed in their present form. These are the provisions that

- include terrorism offenses and computer fraud offenses among the crimes that domestic law enforcement officials can investigate with Title III wiretap and surveillance orders (sections 201 and 202);

- allow domestic law enforcement agents to disclose foreign intelligence information to national security and counter-terrorism officials when the information was acquired by investigative methods not involving a grand jury (sections 203 (b) and (d));

- authorize roving surveillance under FISA (section 206);

- permit investigators to use search warrants, rather than the more rigorous Title III warrants, to seize stored voice mail (section 209);

- permit firms providing communication services to disclose subscriber messages and information voluntarily to law enforcement officials on an emergency basis when necessary to prevent an immediate threat of death or serious physical injury (section 212);

- authorize government investigators, when requested by the victim of a computer attack, to monitor the communications of the computer trespasser (section 217);

- give nationwide effect to judicial orders for the recovery of stored e-mail, regardless of the district in which the judge issuing the order happens to sit (section 220); and

◆   grant private individuals and firms immunity from civil lia-
    bility when they comply with Foreign Intelligence Surveillance
    Court orders to furnish information to the government (sec-
    tion 225).

PEN-REGISTER SURVEILLANCE

There are logical reasons for regulating pen-register surveillance
less strictly than the surveillance of communications content.
Nonetheless, pen registers do raise significant privacy concerns, especially when they are used to trace e-mail and Internet transmissions.
Accordingly, the current, minimal regime of restrictions on pen registers must be strengthened.

The most important weakness in the current system of safeguards is the failure to require that law enforcement officials establish some objective factual basis for this type of surveillance. As a
result, the regime lacks any mechanism for meaningful judicial
review of pen-register applications. The familiar Fourth
Amendment standard of "specific and articulable facts" used in
many other contexts could easily be deployed in the case of pen
registers to meet the need for an operationally workable threshold requirement. There is no reason to think that this modest prerequisite would pose any obstacle to legitimate pen-register
monitoring. Congress should amend both FISA and the domestic
surveillance statutes to require that an application for pen-register
or trap/trace authority set forth specific and articulable facts showing
reasonable grounds to believe that the information sought is relevant
to an ongoing criminal investigation.

Second, pen-register monitoring of Internet usage and private
telephones should not be deployed in the investigation of minor misdemeanors. Congress should limit the use of pen-register and
trap/trace devices to investigation of foreign intelligence crimes and
the serious crimes required to support Title III wiretaps and electronic surveillance.

The Patriot Act's pen-register amendments introduced an
important safeguard by requiring investigators to file with the
court a detailed log of pen-register and trap/trace monitoring, but
this reporting obligation applies only to e-mail and other Internet pen
registers, not to devices used for monitoring the origin and destination

of conventional telephone calls. Congress should extend to telephone pen-register and trap/trace devices the same after-the-fact reporting that is mandated for Internet pen registers and for surveillance of the content of telephone calls.

Finally, there is a pressing need to clarify the distinction between the surveillance of routing information (which is subject to relatively minimal regulation) and the surveillance of content (which is properly subject to more stringent requirements). The Department of Justice should make public the standards it uses to determine what constitutes content, and Congress should formulate a specific definition of "content" for inclusion in the statute itself. In particular, Congress should make clear that search terms transmitted by a computer user are not merely routing information and must be treated as content.

CLANDESTINE SEARCHES

The Patriot Act expanded clandestine search powers in two distinct ways. The first, which has drawn enormous attention and criticism, is the provision that codifies and enlarges the authority to conduct delayed-notification (sneak-and-peek) searches in law enforcement—including ordinary domestic law enforcement. The second, much broader and more dangerous but scarcely noticed, is the provision that permits physical searches under a veil of permanent secrecy in foreign intelligence investigations.

Congress should tighten the delayed notification search powers in ordinary law enforcement (section 213 of the Patriot Act) from several directions. The circumstances now considered sufficient to justify delayed notification are far too broad. Such searches should be permissible in ordinary law enforcement only when immediate notice would endanger a person's life or safety, pose a substantial danger of flight, or present a substantial risk of the destruction of evidence, either by the immediate target of the search or by a confederate. In addition, even when such circumstances apply, the statute should require that notice normally be given within seven days, and courts should be able to authorize extensions or longer initial periods of secrecy only on a "strong showing of necessity."[4] Further, as proposed in several of the pending bills,[5] the attorney general should be directed to issue regular public reports concerning all requests for delayed notification.

Clandestine physical searches in foreign intelligence matters are especially troubling because, under FISA, agents are not obligated to show any need for secrecy, and notification of the search is not merely delayed—normally the homeowner is never notified at all. The absence of a public outcry over these clandestine searches is surprising in light of the intense controversy surrounding the more restricted "delayed notification" searches in ordinary law enforcement.

The lack of public and congressional attention to physical searches under FISA probably can be explained by the fact that the expansion of this power was accomplished indirectly. The Patriot Act did not amend the FISA provisions governing secret physical searches. Instead it enlarged the opportunities to conduct such searches by eliminating the pre–September 11 requirement, applicable to all FISA investigative techniques, that "the purpose" of the investigation must be to gather foreign intelligence. Under the new "significant purpose" language, clandestine FISA searches, like other FISA tools, can now be used even when the primary purpose of the investigation is a criminal prosecution and even when the target of the search is a U.S. citizen. Indeed, Attorney General Ashcroft's 2002 memorandum to implement the new standard, upheld by the Foreign Intelligence Surveillance Court of Review,[6] now gives prosecutors the power to initiate these probes and use them to search American homes secretly, without the showing of necessity that the Fourth Amendment normally would require.*

Although foreign intelligence searches often require secrecy or at least delayed notification, there is no reason to assume that complete secrecy is needed in every case. Congress should permit FISA warrants for physical searches to authorize secrecy only when the necessity for it is demonstrated. Such a requirement can hardly be burdensome since in appropriate cases the demonstration will flow directly from the reasons to suspect espionage or terrorist planning. In addition, Congress should demand that when secrecy is justified, notice must nonetheless be given within a specified period (for example, thirty days in FISA cases), absent a further showing of necessity. Whatever

---

*The Court of Review decision addressed issues involved in electronic surveillance. Much of its logic seems equally applicable to physical searches, but the court might have great reservations about the Ashcroft procedures in that context.

the need for secrecy, eventual notification is an essential safeguard against misuse of the clandestine search power.

FISA ELECTRONIC SURVEILLANCE

The September 11 investigations make clear that the attempt to separate intelligence-gathering functions from law enforcement requires cumbersome structures that will unduly burden our counterterrorism efforts. In dismantling the "wall," however, we must find workable safeguards to replace it. The FISA amendments are among the clearest examples of the Patriot Act's failure to preserve reasonable boundaries and adequate accountability.

Oversight mechanisms for FISA remain feeble. The Intelligence Reform Act of 2004 now mandates disclosure of a few basic statistics,[7] but its reporting requirements are indefensibly narrow and abstract. There is no good reason to excuse the Justice Department from revealing the number of U.S. persons subjected to each type of FISA surveillance.[8] Similarly, the FISA disclosures could easily provide the kinds of aggregate statistics long featured in the government's annual Title III surveillance reports—specifically, the types of locations where surveillance occurred, the average length of initial surveillance and extensions, the number of productive intercepts, and the number of targets subsequently arrested and convicted. Such information by itself cannot begin to ensure sufficient accountability, but there is no plausible danger in revealing it,* and it would at least provide a preliminary basis for public discussion of the FISA powers and the extent to which they are being used properly.

A more effective form of oversight, of course, would be scrutiny on a case-by-case basis by the judge who issues a FISA warrant. FISA,

---

*Department of Justice spokespersons sometimes outdo themselves in suggesting strained rationalizations for secrecy that the Department itself does not consider plausible. At a May 2003 hearing before a House subcommittee, Assistant Attorney General Viet D. Dinh was asked "Why should the number [of FISAs used] be classified?" He responded, "The reason is fairly straightforward. The amount of activity . . . give[s] an insight as to patterns of intelligence and terrorist activities . . . . [Q.] That would tell the enemy something useful . . . ? [A.] Yes, sir." Immediately after this interchange, a Committee member asked another witness, James Dempsey, executive director of the Center for Democracy and Technology, to comment on Dinh's answer.

unlike Title III, does not require investigators who have completed a surveillance to inform the court about the results of their minimization efforts or to describe the extent to which their initial suspicions proved justified. Investigators presumably have to prepare such reports in any event (if not, their procedures are disturbingly lax), and there is no reason to worry that specially selected Foreign Intelligence Surveillance Court judges, who are trusted to issue these warrants in the first place, cannot be trusted to receive and review an end-of-surveillance assessment, redacted if necessary. Now that FISA surveillance is so much more easily authorized and so much more frequently deployed, it becomes especially important to require this additional measure of accountability.

Remedies for abuse are another facet of any effective oversight regime. The existing remedial system for FISA misconduct is woefully inadequate. When individuals face criminal prosecution on the basis of evidence obtained through FISA, their counsel normally ought to be allowed access to the documents necessary to establish whether the procedures were lawful.[9] And unless the circumstances make secrecy imperative, the judge should be required to hold an adversary hearing. (At present, he or she is not even *permitted* to do so, if the attorney general objects.[10])

The problem of weak remedies in the setting of a criminal prosecution is compounded by the fact that individuals *not* subsequently prosecuted—those most likely to have suffered improper surveillance—are even less able to challenge the abuse because they normally will never find out that the details of their private lives had been monitored and recorded for government files.[11] A mechanism for after-the-fact review of unproductive FISA surveillance could be established in the Foreign Intelligence Surveillance Court or in the Justice Department's Office of the Inspector General. Retrospective assessments should not be allowed to create a climate of second-guessing

---

Dempsey replied, "Well, actually Mr. Nadler, the number of FISAs is actually published and known, and we watch how it goes up and down from year to year. . . . I don't think that tells anybody anything . . . in terms of anybody trying to predict where the government is or to try to evade government surveillance." "Anti-Terrorism Investigations and the Fourth Amendment after September 11, 2001," hearing before the Subcommittee on the Constitution, U.S. Congress, House Judiciary Committee, 108th Cong., 1st sess., May 20, 2003, pp. 91–92, available online at http://www .globalsecurity.org/security/library/congress/2003_h/hju87238_0.htm.

that inhibits reasonable intelligence-gathering judgments, but a review mechanism of this sort, capable of notifying most FISA targets at some point after the fact, could identify abusive practices and could afford innocent victims the means of redress that the statutes in theory already provide.

The threshold requirements for FISA electronic surveillance are not dramatically different, in the case of American citizens, from those that apply in ordinary Title III surveillance. Both in effect rest on probable cause to suspect commission of a serious crime.[12] The principal differences between FISA and the Title III regime lie, therefore, in the details of permitted time periods for surveillance, minimization procedures, and other aspects of effective judicial oversight.

For nonresident foreign nationals, however, FISA permits electronic surveillance without probable cause to believe a crime is being committed.[13] A nonresident working for a foreign-based advocacy organization, for example, could easily be subjected to long-term electronic surveillance with limited judicial oversight. True, this broad FISA surveillance power existed before the Patriot Act. But it has become more important and is now subject to greater potential abuse because the Patriot Act allows it to be used by investigators whose primary concern is domestic law enforcement. Indeed, the 2002 Ashcroft memorandum authorizes criminal prosecutors to initiate and control such surveillance.[14] Given the risk of unjustified fishing expeditions under those circumstances, prosecutors should not be allowed to take the lead role in FISA surveillance focused on general foreign policy matters that do not involve suspected espionage, terrorism, or other foreign intelligence crimes.

DOCUMENT DEMANDS

The new document production powers include the government's expanded authority to issue national security letters and the Patriot Act's controversial section 215, which reaches library and bookstore records as well as the membership lists of religious organizations and political advocacy groups. These provisions eliminate virtually all independent oversight, and they do so in an area of sensitive liberties where accountability is exceptionally important.

To restore meaningful safeguards, the first and easiest step is simply to require reasonably informative statistical reporting to Congress. For section 215, existing law does not require the Department of Justice to provide Congress with any details beyond the aggregate number of document production orders obtained, and it does not require any reports at all relating to the use of national security letters or calls for educational records. National security would in no way be compromised, and public awareness as well as accountability would be immeasurably furthered, if Congress simply required the Justice Department to make available aggregate statistics covering the kind of information demanded and the kind of entities from which it was sought. Specifically, semiannual reporting should be mandated with statistics on

- the number of orders applicable to charities, political organizations, religious organizations and their affiliates, libraries, bookstores, and video stores; and

- the number of orders that sought financial transactions, communication records, employment files, membership rolls, contribution lists, medical histories, and educational transcripts.

Another worthwhile step is to eliminate the automatic, indefinite gag order that now accompanies all national security letters and FISA document demands. The government's need for confidentiality can easily be satisfied on a case-by-case basis, whenever the attorney general certifies the need for secrecy, and subpoena recipients should have the right to have gag orders lifted as soon as circumstances permit.

The most important mechanism of accountability, judicial oversight, is now completely inoperative because the only prerequisite for a document demand is the FBI's self-certification that it is acting in good faith. To restore an independent check on abuse of document production powers, it is essential to impose a few simple threshold requirements that would afford a basis for oversight and review by courts. Specifically,

- National security letters, section 215 orders, and demands for educational transcripts should be limited to the records of individuals linked to foreign intelligence crimes. Especially in the case of U.S. citizens or residents, the FBI should be required to certify, as it did before September 11, that the target of the document demand is believed to be a terrorist or the agent of a foreign power.

+ The FBI should likewise be required to certify, again as before September 11, that there are specific and articulable facts to support its suspicions. In sound investigations, FBI agents undoubtedly base their actions on objective data, and orders to produce sensitive documents should not be issued otherwise.

+ The FBI certificate alleging specific and articulable facts should be subject to review by the Foreign Intelligence Surveillance Court. In the absence of exigent circumstances, a judge should determine the sufficiency of the alleged facts, either in all cases or at least when the document production order concerns such sensitive items as medical files, educational transcripts, and records at the core of First Amendment activity (those held by libraries, religious organizations, and political advocacy groups).

+ In the case of applications for orders to produce sensitive records, Congress should enact standards, modeled on those of *NAACP v. Alabama*,[15] obliging investigators to show that the records sought are important (not merely "relevant") to the investigation and that alternative sources of information had been pursued first, whenever possible, in order to minimize the risk to First Amendment rights.

Accountability mechanisms will not interfere with sensible intelligence-gathering efforts. But they would do much to give First Amendment rights more breathing space and to alleviate the kind of public mistrust that the library records provision has fostered.

COMPREHENSIVE OVERSIGHT

As seen throughout this report, the piecemeal mechanisms of accountability already in place are far too weak, even in the narrow domains where they are authorized to operate. That obvious short-coming is compounded by the fact that each of these safeguards is institutionally isolated and limited in its reach. Judicial oversight exercised on a case-by-case basis provides an indispensable means for effective, fact-specific scrutiny. But that strength also is its biggest weakness because a judge concerned only with one case will seldom be in a position to notice troublesome patterns. The judges of the Foreign Intelligence Surveillance Court, a small group of eleven, are more likely to see a significant sample of foreign intelligence surveillance operations, but, even with their wider field of vision, they can easily miss important features of the "big picture."

Beyond that concern, many potentially dangerous practices stemming from the antiterror mission can escape these sorts of oversight altogether. Examples include data-mining procedures in the departments of Defense and Homeland Security, information sharing across agencies, systems to preserve confidentiality and protect the privacy of individuals mentioned in intelligence files, and conduct that may involve direct or indirect forms of racial and ethnic profiling. Existing judicial oversight mechanisms, even if strengthened, provide no substitute for strong, independent institutions with responsibility to make certain that civil liberties considerations are fully respected in the national security and intelligence-gathering efforts of the government as a whole.

With this need in mind, the 9/11 Commission unanimously recommended creation of an agency within the executive branch "to oversee . . . the commitment the government makes to defend our civil liberties."[16] Congress took a step toward implementing that proposal in the 2004 Intelligence Reform Act.[17] The act creates a "civil liberties protection officer" in the Office of the Director of National Intelligence and an "officer for civil rights and civil liberties" in the Department of Homeland Security, each responsible for assessing whether its agency's general policies and actual practices properly respect privacy, civil rights, and civil liberties. A related measure enacted at the end of 2004 provided for a "chief privacy officer" in each agency having law enforcement or antiterrorism responsibilities.[18] The Intelligence Reform Act also created a Civil Liberties Oversight Board in the Executive Office of the President, charged with providing advice to the president on the development and implementation of national security policies that affect privacy and civil liberties.[19]

These measures move in the right direction but are at best only a beginning. The privacy and civil-liberties officers report to superiors in their respective agencies. Their effectiveness as a counterweight to operating officials within their agencies will inevitably be small to nonexistent in the absence of public and congressional support. Yet, their authority to make their concerns public is vague and at best limited.[20]

Of perhaps greater concern, the centerpiece of the oversight effort, the new Privacy and Civil Liberties Oversight Board in the Executive Office of the President, emerged from Congress in greatly weakened form. The intelligence reform bill that passed the Senate in October 2004 included a detailed package of features designed to guarantee the board's independence, status, and information-gathering capabilities. But the elements most essential to its ability to function successfully were systematically watered down in conference to accommodate the misgivings of representatives from the House.

As enacted, the final intelligence reform legislation creates a board that has no independence whatever, has limited ability to gather information, and does not even have the right to be consulted about privacy and civil liberties matters within its purview.[21] It is required to report annually to Congress on its "major activities,"[22] but there is no mandate to disclose minority views or to describe the board's findings in any specific area.

With respect to its independence, only two of the board's five members (the chair and vice-chair) must be confirmed by the Senate. None of them need be a member of the minority party, all of them can be appointed to serve on a part-time basis, and all of them hold their positions at the pleasure of the president.

The board's investigatory powers are weak. It has no subpoena power, and, although its members must have security clearances, its information-gathering functions are entirely dependent on the voluntary cooperation of the agencies it oversees.* Its position is no better when it needs information from outside contractors—a group whose actions are increasingly important, given present enthusiasm for outsourcing law enforcement functions to private security firms.

---

*The act requires that the head of each agency "shall ensure compliance" with board requests for any information that "may be provided to the board in accordance with applicable law." §1061(d)(3). But the act gives the board no mechanism to challenge an agency's determination that applicable law prevents disclosure and no remedy if the head of the agency is uncooperative or dilatory.

If such contractors are uncooperative, the board can request that the attorney general seek a subpoena, but the decision whether to pursue the matter is left entirely to the attorney general's discretion.* Again, the board's ability to function depends on the Justice Department's cooperation, a potentially fatal prerequisite for an agency whose mission is oversight of the law enforcement establishment. It faces another barrier as well because the Intelligence Reform Act authorizes the national intelligence director and the attorney general to block disclosure to the board, despite the security clearances of its members, whenever necessary to protect national security or "sensitive" law enforcement information. Information can be withheld not only when it involves ongoing investigations but also when it concerns only broad policy matters.[23]

Left with the worst of both worlds, the new Privacy and Civil Liberties Oversight Board has none of the broad information-gathering powers that an in-house oversight authority typically enjoys and none of the independence that would come from its being situated partly or entirely outside the executive branch. This is little more than "oversight" in name only.

A strong, independent oversight agency remains essential. Only a profound distaste for checks and balances can explain Congress's failure to create one. Practicable mechanisms are readily available. Indeed, an earlier version of the 2004 act spelled them out in detail, in a form sufficiently balanced to win approval in the Senate. That bill would have ensured the board a substantial degree of independence. It would have given it the ability to overcome all too predictable resistance from executive officials who want to exercise power unilaterally and do not want their actions scrutinized, even when (or particularly when) civil liberties may hang in the balance.

To be sure, too much second-guessing can demoralize an agency, and sanctions for missteps can be overdone. A permanent special prosecutor for civil-liberties infractions could prompt excessive aversion to risk within the intelligence community and thus might exacerbate one of the major problems identified by the 9/11 Commission.[24] But the opposite extreme—broad FBI powers with no

---

*When the board requests Justice Department assistance in obtaining information from parties outside the executive branch, "the Attorney General *shall* review the request and *may* take such steps as appropriate to ensure compliance with the request for the information." §1061(d)(2)(B) (emphasis added).

practically operative check—is equally dangerous, as the commission recognized in urging creation of an effective oversight board.

The remedy for current inadequacies of the Privacy and Civil Liberties Oversight Board could take a variety of equally effective forms. Congress has considerable room to discuss and fine-tune the details, so long as the final package provides realistic guarantees for the board's independence, information-gathering power, and ability to communicate with Capitol Hill.

To secure the board's independence, there ought to be a full-time chair and vice-chair from opposing parties and a requirement that no more than three of the five members belong to the same political party. Senate confirmation for all five members should be part of the process. While it is reasonable to grant the president the prerogative to designate the chair, all members should be appointed for fixed periods (for example, staggered six-year tenures) terminable only for cause.

For an effective board, subpoena power not dependent on Justice Department approval is essential. National security concerns can be met simply by retaining the security clearance requirement and by preserving (perhaps in narrower form) the existing procedure for blocking disclosure of sensitive information. To ensure that oversight does not foster excessive caution among investigators, Congress could consider making explicit that the board's concern is not with matters of individual discipline. Presumably, information disclosed to it could normally be redacted to remove details that identify individual officers, leaving disciplinary concerns to the inspectors general of the respective agencies.

Sensitive matters before the board need not be revealed to Congress in all their detail, of course. Alternatively, the board might be directed to disclose certain sensitive matters but only to select congressional committees, as the intelligence community does now, with assurance that only redacted versions will be made public. Either way, the topics that the board must cover in its reports need to be spelled out. They should include not only the vaguely worded "major activities" but also such crucial matters as the board's findings and recommendations on all issues reviewed, minority views if any, and the nature of any programs and practices that were instituted or retained against its advice. Material of that nature often will have to be described in redacted form. But there is no justification for assuming, as the current statute does, that a board, serving at the president's pleasure, should share with Congress and the public only what little information it may choose to reveal about the civil liberties problems it encounters. A presumption in favor of disclosure and public discussion when feasible would be an important step in the direction of accountability and public trust.

An oversight board reconstituted in these ways is easily achievable at little cost. It would become an essential part of the effective system of checks and balances that the 9/11 Commission urged the nation to institute.

THE LONG HAUL

If America continues to succumb to seductive calls for unquestioning deference to the "commander-in-chief," if we allow unrestricted executive powers to grow, and if at the same time we remain inattentive to the resource deficits and organizational weaknesses that continue to plague our intelligence-gathering operations, then this country cannot ever be safe, no matter how much liberty its citizens are willing to sacrifice.

If, however, Americans approach the problem of terrorism with awareness of its complexities, remembering how easily an overbroad power can backfire, and if we are willing to balance strong investigative powers with effective mechanisms of oversight and accountability, then—and only then—can our nation have a vigorous and successful counterterrorism strategy that does not put the core liberties of a free society at risk.

NOTES

CHAPTER 1

1. *The 9/11 Commission Report: Final Report of the National Commission on Terrorist Attacks upon the United States* (New York: W. W. Norton and Company, n.d.), p. 394, available online at http://www.9-11commission.gov/report/911Report.pdf.

2. Provisionally titled *To Deter and Punish Terrorist Acts in the United States and around the World, to Enhance Law Enforcement Investigatory Tools, and for Other Purposes,* HR 2975, 107th Cong., 1st sess., *Congressional Record* 147, no. 130 (October 2, 2001): H 6135. A substitute version, HR 3162, was the bill ultimately enacted as the *USA PATRIOT Act.*

3. See Beryl A. Howell, "Seven Weeks: The Making of the USA PATRIOT Act," 72 *George Washington Law Review* 1145 (2004).

4. *Uniting and Strengthening America by Providing Appropriate Tools Required to Intercept and Obstruct Terrorism (USA PATRIOT) Act,* Public Law 107-56, *U.S. Statutes at Large* 115 (2001).

5. Ibid., §412(a).

6. See Stephen J. Schulhofer, *The Enemy Within: Intelligence Gathering, Law Enforcement, and Civil Liberties in the Wake of September 11* (New York: The Century Foundation Press, 2002), pp. 15–16.

7. *USA PATRIOT Act,* §423.

8. Ibid., §421(b)(1)(B)(ii).

9. Ibid., §§103, 205, 404, 414, 501–2, 611–24, 816.

10. Ibid., §§203, 504, 701, 905, 908.

11. Ibid., §1012.

12. Ibid., §1016.

13. Ibid., §§802, 810–11.

14. Ibid., §805; see *Humanitarian Law Project v. Ashcroft,* 309 F. Supp. 2nd 1185, 1198 (C.D. Cal. 2004) (terms "expert advice or assistance"

added by *USA PATRIOT Act* §805 are unconstitutionally vague). Cf. *Humanitarian Law Project v. Reno*, 205 F. 3rd 1130, 1137–38 (9th Cir. 2000) (terms "training" and "personnel" are unconstitutionally vague); *United States v. Sattar*, 272 F. Supp. 2nd 348, 358 (S.D. N.Y. 2003) (terms "training" and "communications equipment" are unconstitutionally vague). Cf. *United States v. Lindh*, 212 F. Supp. 2nd 541, 574 (E.D. Va. 2002) (terms "services" and "personnel" are not unconstitutionally vague); *United States v. Goba*, 220 F. Supp. 2nd 182, 194 (W.D. N.Y. 2002) (terms "training" and "personnel" are not unconstitutionally vague); *United States v. Khan*, 309 F. Supp. 2nd 789, 822 (E.D. Va. 2004) ("personnel" is not unconstitutionally vague, as applied to defendants who would have served a terrorist organization as "soldiers, recruiters, and procurers of supplies").

15. *USA PATRIOT Act,* §1007.

16. Ibid., §§413–18.

17. Ibid., §§311–77.

18. See Schulhofer, *Enemy Within,* pp. 52–54.

19. *Intelligence Reform and Terrorism Prevention Act of 2004,* Public Law 108-458, *U.S. Statutes at Large* 118 (2004): 3638, §6001(a), amending *U.S. Code* 50, §1801(b)(1).

20. Ibid., §6001.

21. Ibid., §6604.

22. Ibid., §6952.

23. Ibid., §§7208–13.

24. Ibid., §6003.

25. Ibid., §§1061, 8304–5.

26. *USA PATRIOT Act,* §§ 204 (a purely technical amendment, attempting to tighten the links among the distinct surveillance regimes), 205 (translators), 208 (judges), 222 (compensation). In addition, §221, though included in Title II (the surveillance procedures section of the Patriot Act), addresses trade sanctions against state sponsors of terrorism; it does not deal with surveillance procedures at all.

27. Ibid., §§ 206, 207, 214, 218, and 225. These provisions are analyzed in Chapter 3 of this report.

28. Ibid., §215, discussed in Chapter 4 of this report.

29. The provisions dealing with conventional law enforcement powers are discussed in Chapter 5 of this report.

30. *9/11 Commission Report,* p. 394 (emphasis added).

31. See "The USA Patriot Act: Myth vs. Reality," U.S. Department of Justice, September 2003, pp. 22, 23, available online at http://www.nunes.house.gov/PatriotAct.htm.

32. *Marab v. IDF Commander in the West Bank,* Israel High Court of Justice, HCJ 3239/02, February 5, 2003, ¶35.

CHAPTER 2

1. *Hamdi v. Rumsfeld,* 124 S. Ct. 2633, 2650 (2004) (plurality opinion).

2. James Risen and David Johnston, "F.B.I. Report Found Agency Not Ready to Counter Terror," *New York Times,* June 1, 2002, p. A1.

3. Ibid.

4. Patrick Leahy, Charles Grassley, and Arlen Specter, "FBI Oversight in the 107th Congress by the Senate Judiciary Committee: FISA Implementation Failures" (hereafter cited as "Senate Oversight Report"), interim report, February 2003, available online at http://leahy.senate.gov/press/200302 /FISA02-03.html.

5. Ibid., p. 26.

6. Ibid., pp. 32–33. For detail on the FBI's information technology problems, see U.S. Department of Justice, Office of the Inspector General, *The Federal Bureau of Investigation's Efforts to Improve the Sharing of Intelligence and Other Information,* Audit Report 04-10, December 2003, p. iii, available online at http://www.justice.gov/oig/audit/FBI/0410/final.pdf.

7. "FBI Intelligence Investigations: Coordination within Justice on Counterintelligence Criminal Matters Is Limited," report to the ranking minority member, Committee on Governmental Affairs, U.S. Senate, GAO-01-780, U.S. General Accounting Office, July 2001, available online at http://www.gao.gov/new.items/d01780.pdf.

8. Ibid., p. 3.

9. Ibid., p. 30.

10. Ibid., p. 5.

11. Ibid., p. 33.

12. Ibid., p. 33 (emphasis added).

13. *The 9/11 Commission Report: Final Report of the National Commission on Terrorist Attacks upon the United States* (New York: W. W. Norton and Company, n.d.), p. 257, available online at http://www .9-11commission.gov/report/911Report.pdf.

14. Ibid., pp. 259, 277.

15. Don Van Natta, Jr., and David Johnston, "Wary of Risk, Slow to Adapt, F.B.I. Stumbles in Terror War," *New York Times,* June 2, 2002, sec. I, pp. 1, 31.

16. Statement of Mary Jo White, former U.S. attorney for the Southern District of New York, before the Joint Intelligence Committees, U.S. Congress, "Joint Inquiry into the September 11th Terrorist Attacks," 108th Cong., 2nd sess., October 8, 2002, text available online at http://intelli-gence.senate.gov/0210hrg/021008/white.pdf.

17. *9/11 Commission Report,* pp. 268–69.

18. Ibid., p. 539, n. 83.

19. The episode is described in detail in *Joint Inquiry into Intelligence Community Activities before and after the Terrorist Attacks of September 11,*

2001: *Report of the U.S. Senate Select Committee on Intelligence and U.S. House Permanent Select Committee on Intelligence,* S. Rept. 107-351, 107th Cong., 2nd sess., December 2002, pp. 315–24, available online at http://a257.g.akamaitech.net/7/257/2422/24jul20031400/www.gpoaccess.gov/serialset/creports/pdf/fullreport_errata.pdf; Senate Oversight Report, supra note 4, pp. 15–17, 22–23.

20. *9/11 Commission Report,* pp. 76–77.

21. *Intelligence Activities and the Rights of Americans: Final Report of the Select Committee to Study Governmental Operations with Respect to Intelligence Activities,* vol. II: *Intelligence Activities and the Rights of Americans* (hereafter cited as "Church Committee Report"), S. Rept. 94-755, 94th Cong., 2nd sess., April 26, 1976, pp. 2–3, n. 5 (emphasis added).

22. Ibid., pp. 7–10.

23. Ibid., pp. 4, 5.

24. Ibid., p. 4.

25. Ibid., p. 6.

26. Ibid., p. 17.

27. *United States v. United States District Court* (also known as the *Keith* case), 407 U.S. 297, 313 (1972).

28. "House of the Rising Farce," *Economist,* June 15, 2002, p. 30.

29. Church Committee Report, supra note 21, p. 14.

30. See Stephen J. Schulhofer, *The Enemy Within: Intelligence Gathering, Law Enforcement, and Civil Liberties in the Wake of September 11* (New York: The Century Foundation Press, 2002), p. 52.

31. See *Uniting and Strengthening America by Providing Appropriate Tools Required to Intercept and Obstruct Terrorism (USA PATRIOT) Act,* Public Law 107-56, *U.S. Statutes at Large* 115 (2001): 272, §366.

32. See, e.g., U.S. Department of Justice, *Federal Bureau of Investigation's Efforts to Improve the Sharing of Intelligence;* John Schwartz and Lowell Bergman, "F.B.I. Sees Delay in New Network to Oversee Cases," *New York Times,* June 26, 2004, p. A1, summarizing some of the recent efforts made but reporting that, according to FBI officials, "they would not be able to fully deploy a long-awaited computer system to manage the bureau's case files before the end of the year as promised, and that they could not predict when the entire system would be in place."

33. Eric Lichtblau, "F.B.I. Said to Lag on Translations of Terror Tapes," *New York Times,* September 27, 2004, p. A1.

Chapter 3

1. *Foreign Intelligence Surveillance Act,* Public Law 95-511, *U.S. Statutes at Large* 92 (1978): 1783, codified at *U.S. Code* 50, §1801 et seq.

2. U.S. Constitution, amend. 4.

3. See, e.g., *Chimel v. California*, 395 U.S. 752 (1969).

4. *Illinois v. Gates*, 462 U.S. 213, 238 (1983).

5. U.S. Constitution, amend. 4.

6. See *Coolidge v. New Hampshire*, 403 U.S. 443 (1971).

7. Ibid.

8. *United States v. United States District Court*, 407 U.S. 297 (1972), named the *Keith* case after Judge Damon J. Keith, who issued the original decision.

9. Ibid., at 320.

10. Ibid., at 314.

11. U.S. Constitution, amend. 4.

12. *Berger v. New York*, 388 U.S. 41 (1967).

13. *Omnibus Crime Control and Safe Streets Act*, Public Law 90-351, Title III, *U.S. Statutes at Large* 82 (1986): 197, codified at *U.S. Code* 18 (1968), §2510 et seq.

14. Ibid., §§2516–19.

15. Ibid., §2511(3).

16. *United States v. United States District Court*, at 310–11 and n. 10.

17. Ibid., at 309, n. 8.

18. Ibid., at 320–21.

19. *Foreign Intelligence Surveillance Act*.

20. Ibid., §1805(a)(3).

21. Ibid., §1801(b)(2).

22. Ibid., §1804(a)(7)(B).

23. *United States v. Pelton*, 835 F. 2nd 1067, 1075 (4th Cir. 1987).

24. See "Foreign Intelligence Surveillance Act Orders 1979–2002," Electronic Privacy Information Center, Washington, D.C., last updated May 6, 2003, available online at http://www.epic.org/privacy/wiretap/stats/fisa_stats.html. By comparison, the federal courts receive on average roughly 1,175 ordinary electronic surveillance warrant applications per year. See "2003 Wiretap Report," Administrative Office of the United States Courts, April 2004, p. 32, Table 7, available online at http://www.uscourts.gov/wiretap03/contents.html.

25. "Foreign Intelligence Surveillance Act Orders," supra note 24.

26. E.g., ibid.

27. See *The 9/11 Commission Report: Final Report of the National Commission on Terrorist Attacks upon the United States* (New York: W. W. Norton and Company, n.d.), pp. 78–80, available online at http://www.9-11commission.gov/report/911Report.pdf; *Joint Inquiry into Intelligence Community Activities before and after the Terrorist Attacks of September 11, 2001: Report of the U.S. Senate Select Committee on Intelligence and U.S. House Permanent Select Committee on Intelligence*, S. Rept. 107-351, 107th Cong., 2nd sess., December 2002, pp. 363–68, available online at http://a257.g.akamaitech.net/7/257/2422/24jul20031400/www.gpoaccess.gov/serialset/creports/pdf/fullreport_errata.pdf.

28. *Joint Inquiry into Intelligence Community Activities,* pp. 363–64.

29. Patrick Leahy, Charles Grassley, and Arlen Specter, "FBI Oversight in the 107th Congress by the Senate Judiciary Committee: FISA Implementation Failures" (hereafter cited as "Senate Oversight Report"), interim report, February 2003, available online at http://leahy.senate.gov/press/200302 /FISA02-03.html.

30. Ibid., p. 22.

31. Ibid., pp. 17–25. See also the FBI's April 2000 memorandum acknowledging that an OIPR official, unhappy with errors in the FBI's counterterrorism surveillance, has complained about the "inability on the part of the FBI to manage its FISAs." Quoted in Stephen J. Schulhofer, *The Enemy Within: Intelligence Gathering, Law Enforcement, and Civil Liberties in the Wake of September 11* (New York: The Century Foundation Press, 2002), p. 33.

32. Senate Oversight Report, supra note 29, p. 22.

33. Quoted in Senate Oversight Report, supra note 29, p. 28.

34. See *Joint Inquiry into Intelligence Community Activities,* pp. 315–24; Senate Oversight Report, supra note 29, pp. 15–17, 22–23.

35. *Joint Inquiry into Intelligence Community Activities,* p. 321.

36. *Foreign Intelligence Surveillance Act,* §§1801(a)(4); 1801(b)(2)(C),(E) (2003). See Senate Oversight Report, supra note 29, p. 22 (concluding that FBI misinterpretation of these FISA provisions was inexplicable and indefensible).

37. In December 2004 FISA's definition of "agent of a foreign power" was extended to include non-U.S. persons who engage in or prepare to engage in international terrorism, whether or not they are acting on behalf of a foreign power or a foreign terrorist organization. See *Intelligence Reform and Terrorism Prevention Act of 2004,* Public Law 108-458, *U.S. Statutes at Large* 118 (2004): 3638, §6001(a), amending *U.S. Code 50,* §1801(b)(1). The new provision sunsets on December 31, 2005. See §6001(b).

38. *Foreign Intelligence Surveillance Act,* §1804(a)(7)(B) (emphasis added).

39. *Foreign Intelligence Surveillance Act,* §§1801(h), 1804(a)(5), 1805(a)(4).

40. See *In re Sealed Case,* 310 F. 3rd 717, 727 (Foreign Intel. Surv. Ct. Rev. 2002).

41. *Foreign Intelligence Surveillance Act,* §§1801(h)(3), 1806.

42. Courts did allow use of FISA procedures even when foreign intelligence gathering was not the government's sole purpose—for example, when agents pursuing a foreign intelligence inquiry could anticipate from the outset the possibility of using the fruits of surveillance in a criminal trial. *United States v. Duggan,* 743 F. 2nd 59, 78 (2nd Cir. 1984). But FISA surveillance

remained legitimate only when foreign intelligence gathering was the agents' primary purpose.

43. See *In re Sealed Case*, at 728; *In re All Matters Submitted to the Foreign Intelligence Surveillance Court*, 218 F. Supp. 2nd 611, 619 (Foreign Intel. Surv. Ct., 2002).

44. *9/11 Commission Report*, pp. 78–79.

45. *In re All Matters Submitted to the Foreign Intelligence Surveillance Court*, at 619.

46. Ibid.; *In re Sealed Case*, at 728.

47. *9/11 Commission Report*, p. 79.

48. *In re All Matters Submitted to the Foreign Intelligence Surveillance Court*, at 620.

49. Ibid., at 620–21.

50. *Joint Inquiry into Intelligence Community Activities*, p. 367.

51. See statement of Patrick Fitzgerald, U.S. attorney for the Northern District of Illinois, before the Judiciary Committee, U.S. Congress, Senate, in hearings on "Protecting Our National Security from Terrorist Attacks: A Review of Criminal Terrorism Investigations and Prosecutions," October 21, 2003, text available online at http://judiciary.senate.gov/testimony.cfm?id=965&wit_id=2741.

52. Ibid.

53. See Senate Oversight Report, supra note 29, p. 31.

54. *Uniting and Strengthening America by Providing Appropriate Tools Required to Intercept and Obstruct Terrorism (USA PATRIOT) Act*, Public Law 107-56, *U.S. Statutes at Large* 115 (2001): 272, §504.

55. *Foreign Intelligence Surveillance Act*, §1804(a)(7)(B), as amended by *USA PATRIOT Act*, §218 (emphasis added).

56. See Beryl Howell, "FISA: Has the Solution Become a Problem?" in *Protecting What Matters: Technology, Liberty, and Security since 9/11*, ed. Clayton Northouse (forthcoming, 2005).

57. *USA PATRIOT Act*, §224.

58. *Omnibus Crime Control and Safe Streets Act*, Title III, 2518 (11) (b).

59. U.S. Constitution, amend. 4. For such a challenge, see, e.g., Tracey Maclin, "Amending the Fourth: Another Grave Threat to Liberty," *National Law Journal*, November 12, 2001, p. A20.

60. The Supreme Court so held in *Olmstead v. United States*, 277 U.S. 438 (1928).

61. *Katz v. United States*, 389 U.S. 347 (1967).

62. *USA PATRIOT Act*, §207(a)(2). The caption of this section refers to "Surveillance of Non-United States Persons," but the language extending the period for physical searches amends a section of FISA that applies to American citizens as well.

63. *Omnibus Crime Control and Safe Streets Act*, Title III, §2518(4)(e)(5).

64. See, e.g., *United States v. Johns,* 948 F. 2nd 599 (9th Cir. 1991); *United States v. Freitas,* 800 F. 2nd 1451 (9th Cir. 1986).

65. See *Foreign Intelligence Surveillance Act,* §1825(b) and (d). Under these provisions notification is required only when the government intends to use the fruits of such a search as evidence in a formal trial or hearing. In addition, notification is permitted in the case of the clandestine search of the residence of a U.S. person but, even then, only if the attorney general determines that "there is no national security interest in continuing to maintain the secrecy of the search."

66. Letter from Assistant Attorney General William E. Moschella to L. Ralph Mecham, director, Administrative Office of the United States Courts, April 30, 2004.

67. Ibid.

68. See "2003 Wiretap Report," p. 32, Table 4. From a total of 486 in 2001, approvals of federal warrant applications rose to 497 in 2002 and to 578 in 2003.

69. See *In re All Matters Submitted to the Foreign Intelligence Surveillance Court,* at 622.

70. For U.S. persons suspected of foreign intelligence crimes, electronic surveillance can last for ninety days (three times the period allowed in investigating domestic crime), there is only minimal judicial control of particularity and the scope of surveillance, and clandestine physical searches (normally impermissible in investigating domestic crime) are allowed for ninety-day periods with little showing of special need.

71. See *Foreign Intelligence Surveillance Act,* §§1806(e) and (f), 1810.

72. See ibid., §§1825, 1828.

73. Memorandum, Office of the Attorney General, March 6, 2002, available online at http://www.fas.org/irp/agency/doj/fisa/ag030602.html, quoted in *In re All Matters Submitted to the Foreign Intelligence Surveillance Court,* at 615 n. 2 (emphasis in original).

74. *In re All Matters Submitted to the Foreign Intelligence Surveillance Court,* at 623.

75. Ibid., at 626 (emphasis added).

76. Ibid., at 526–27 (emphasis added).

77. Ibid., at 624.

78. *In re Sealed Case,* at 717, 735.

79. Ibid., at 736.

80. Ibid., at 731, 733–34.

81. *Intelligence Reform and Terrorism Prevention Act,* §6001.

82. *Foreign Intelligence Surveillance Act,* §1801(b)(1)(C), as amended, 2004.

83. *Joint Inquiry into Intelligence Community Activities,* p. 321; Senate Oversight Report, supra note 29, pp. 20–23.

84. Senate Oversight Report, supra note 29, pp. 29–30.

85. See, e.g., the resolution adopted by the American Bar Association at its midyear meeting in Seattle, February 10, 2003, available online at http://www.epic.org/privacy/terrorism/fisa/aba_res_021003.html; proposed *Domestic Surveillance Oversight Act of 2003*, S 436, 108th Cong., 1st sess., *Congressional Record* 149, no. 30 (February 25, 2003): S 2705, Title VI.

86. See proposed *Civil Liberties Restoration Act*, S 2528, 108th Cong., 2nd sess., *Congressional Record* 150, no. 83 (June 16, 2004): S6893–94, §401.

87. Senate Oversight Report, supra note 29, p. 7.

88. See Ibid., pp. 1, 10–11, 35–36.

89. *Foreign Intelligence Surveillance Act*, §1805(e)(3).

90. See ibid., §1807. More detailed information is provided on a confidential basis to the House and Senate Select Committees on Intelligence. Refer to §1808.

91. E.g., "2003 Wiretap Report."

92. *Intelligence Reform and Terrorism Prevention Act*, §6002. The provision was apparently based on the proposed *Domestic Surveillance Oversight Act*, but, unlike that bill, it does not require disclosure of the number of U.S. persons targeted by FISA surveillance.

93. See Howell, "FISA: Has the Solution Become a Problem?"

94. *Foreign Intelligence Surveillance Act*, §§1806(e), 1825(f).

95. See Howell, "FISA: Has the Solution Become a Problem?"

96. Amendments along these lines are incorporated in the proposed *Civil Liberties Restoration Act*, §401.

97. See *Classified Information Procedures Act*, Public Law 96-456, *U.S. Statutes at Large* 94 (1980): 2025, codified at *U.S Code* 18 App. 3, §4.

98. See *In re Sealed Case*, at 735–36.

99. *Foreign Intelligence Surveillance Act*, §§1801(b)(1)(A), 1801(e)(2)(B), 1804(a)(4).

100. Ibid., §1801(e)(2)(B).

101. *In re Sealed Case*, at 736.

102. See supra note 65.

103. *Foreign Intelligence Surveillance Act*, §§1801(b)(2), 1821(1), 1824(a)(3).

CHAPTER 4

1. *United States v. Morton Salt Co.*, 338 U.S. 632, 651–52 (1950).

2. *Stoner v. California*, 376 U.S. 483 (1964).

3. *Chapman v. United States*, 365 U.S. 610 (1961).

4. E.g., *United States v. Miller*, 425 U.S. 435 (1976); *Smith v. Maryland*, 442 U.S. 735 (1979).

5. *Currency and Foreign Transactions Reporting Act,* Public Law 91-508, Title I, *U.S. Statutes at Large* 84 (1970): 1116, codified at U.S. Code 12, §1951 et seq.; *Right to Financial Privacy Act,* Public Law 95-630, Title XI, *U.S. Statutes at Large* 92 (1978): 3697, codified at *U.S. Code* 12, §3401 et seq.; *General Education Provisions Act,* Public Law 90-247, Title IV, *U.S. Statutes at Large* 81 (1968): 814, codified at *U.S. Code* 20, §1232g; see *McDonough v. Widnall,* 891 F. Supp. 1439 (D. Colo. 1995) (The Right to Financial Privacy Act was passed by Congress "in order to . . . fill in a void left by the Supreme Court's holding in *United States v. Miller*").

6. *Right to Financial Privacy Act,* §3410(c).

7. *General Education Provisions Act,* §1232g(b).

8. *Foreign Intelligence Surveillance Act,* Public Law 95-511, *U.S. Statutes at Large* 92 (1978): 1783, codified at *U.S. Code* 50, §1862(b)(2) (2000 ed.).

9. Ibid.

10. *Right to Financial Privacy Act,* §3414(a)(5)(A) (1978, 1982, 1986).

11. *Electronic Communications Privacy Act,* Public Law 99-508, Title II, *U.S. Statutes at Large* 100 (1986): 1867, codified at *U.S. Code* 18, §2709(b); *Right to Financial Privacy Act,* §3414; *Fair Credit Reporting Act,* Public Law 91-508, *U.S. Statutes at Large* 84 (1970): 1114, codified at *U.S. Code* 15, §1681.

12. *Doe v. Ashcroft,* 2004 U.S. Dist. LEXIS 19343 (S.D.N.Y., Sept. 28, 2004).

13. See ibid., at *27.

14. *Right to Financial Privacy Act,* §§3414(a)(1)(C); 3414(a)(5)(A) (2001) (emphasis added); *Electronic Communications Privacy Act,* §2709(b) (2001), as amended by *Uniting and Strengthening America by Providing Appropriate Tools Required to Intercept and Obstruct Terrorism (USA PATRIOT) Act,* Public Law 107-56, *U.S. Statutes at Large* 115 (2001): 272, §505(a).

15. *Family Educational Rights and Privacy Act,* Public Law 93-380, *U.S. Statutes at Large* 88 (1974): 571, codified at *U.S. Code* 20, §1232g(j)(1) and (2) (2001), as amended by *USA PATRIOT Act,* §507 (2001).

16. Ibid. The amended FERPA provisions still require a court order, and the official seeking the order must "certify that there are specific and artic-ulable facts giving reason to believe that the educational records are likely to contain [relevant] information." But once the court determines that the application contains the required certification, it must issue the order; it cannot examine the factual specifics or assess their adequacy.

17. *Currency and Foreign Transactions Reporting Act,* Title II, *U.S. Statutes at Large* 84 (1970): 1118, codified at *U.S. Code* 31, §5312 (2003); *Right to Financial Privacy Act,* as amended by *Intelligence Authorization Act,* Public Law 108-177, *U.S. Statutes at Large* 117 (2003): 2599.

18. *Foreign Intelligence Surveillance Act,* §1861(a)(1) (2001), as amended by *USA PATRIOT Act,* §215 (2001).

19. See FBI memorandum, "SAMPLE FISA Business Record Request," April 14, 2003, available online at http://www.epic.org/privacy/terrorism/usapatriot/foia/FBIemail.pdf.

20. See pp. 67–71, infra.

21. *USA PATRIOT Act,* §§215; 505(a)(2)(B) and (3)(B); 505(b)(2) (2001) (emphasis added).

22. Dan Eggen, "Ashcroft: Patriot Act Provision Unused," *Washington Post,* September 18, 2003, p. A13.

23. See documents released in response to a Freedom of Information Act order, American Civil Liberties Union, New York, August 2004, available online at http://www.aclu.org/patriotfoia; "New Records Show that FBI Invoked Controversial Surveillance Powers Weeks after Attorney General Declared that Power Had Never Been Used," press release, American Civil Liberties Union, New York, June 17, 2004, available online at www.aclu.org/news//NewsPrint.cfm?ID=15959&c=262.

24. See Dan Eggen and Robert O'Harrow, Jr., "U.S. Steps Up Secret Surveillance," *Washington Post,* March 24, 2003, p. A1; "List of National Security Letters Issued by FBI between October 26, 2001, and January 21, 2003," American Civil Liberties Union, New York, January 2003, available online at http://www.aclu.org/patriot_foia/FOIA/NSLlists.pdf.

25. *Olmstead v. United States,* 277 U.S. 438, 478 (1928) (dissenting opinion).

26. Quoted in Zenaida A. Gonzalez, "FBI Can Request Library Logs," *Florida Today* (Melbourne, Fla.), September 23, 2002, p. 1.

27. *NAACP v. Alabama,* 357 U.S. 449 (1958).

28. Ibid., at 461–63.

29. See, e.g., *Communist Party v. Subversive Activities Control Board,* 367 U.S. 1 (1961); *New York ex rel. Bryant v. Zimmerman,* 278 U.S. 63 (1928).

30. *Gibson v. Florida Legislative Investigation Committee,* 372 U.S. 539 (1963).

31. *Electronic Communications Privacy Act,* §2709(b) (2001), as amended by *USA PATRIOT Act,* §505(a) (2001); *Family Educational Rights and Privacy Act,* §1232g(j)(1)(A), added by *USA PATRIOT Act,* §507 (2001).

32. *Foreign Intelligence Surveillance Act,* §1861(b)(2), as amended by *USA PATRIOT Act,* §215; *Right to Financial Privacy Act,* §3414(a)(5)(A) (2001), as amended by *USA PATRIOT Act,* §505(b) (2001); *Fair Credit Reporting Act,* §1681u(a)(B), (b)(B), and (c)(B) (2001), as amended by *USA PATRIOT Act,* §505(c) (2001).

33. *Foreign Intelligence Surveillance Act,* §1862(b).

34. Ibid., §1861(d).

35. Moreover, this skeletal public reporting requirement is not supplemented, as it is in the case of electronic surveillance (*Foreign Intelligence*

Surveillance Act, §1808), physical searches (§1826), and pen-register surveillance (§1846), by detailed, semiannual reporting on a confidential basis to the House and Senate Select Committees on Intelligence.

36. Quoted in Gonzalez, "FBI Can Request Library Logs."

37. Quoted in Diana Graettinger, "Official Counters Patriot Act Critics," *Bangor Daily News,* April 4, 2003, p. 1.

38. Ibid. See also Bob Egelko and Maria Alicia Gaura, "Libraries Post Patriot Act Warnings; Santa Cruz Branches Tell Patrons that FBI May Spy on Them," *San Francisco Chronicle,* March, 10, 2003, p. A1 (quoting Corallo as stating that "the idea that any American citizen can have their [library or bookstore] records checked by the FBI, that's not true").

39. "Viet Dinh and Marc Rotenberg Debate Patriot Act," National Press Club, Washington, D.C., April 24, 2003, video available online at http://www.c-span.org.

40. Timothy Burgess, U.S. attorney for the District of Alaska, testimony on House Joint Resolution no. 22, "Patriot Act and Defending Civil Liberties," State Legislature of Alaska, 23rd Legislature, 1st sess., May 13, 2003, text available online at http://www.legis.state.ak.us.

41. Quoted in Egelko and Gaura, "Libraries Post Patriot Act Warnings."

42. Quoted in Elizabeth Wolfe, "Library Surveillance Exclusion Sought," Associated Press, March 6, 2003, available online at http://www .govtech.net/news.

43. *USA PATRIOT Act,* §§215, 505, 507.

44. "National Security Letter Matters," memorandum to all field offices from the Office of General Counsel, Federal Bureau of Investigation, November 28, 2001, disclosed in response to Freedom of Information Act litigation by the American Civil Liberties Union, available online at http://www.aclu.org /patriot_foia/FOIA/Nov2001FBImemo.pdf (emphasis added).

45. "The USA Patriot Act: Myth vs. Reality," U.S. Department of Justice, September 2003, p. 14, available online at http://www.nunes.house.gov /PatriotAct.htm.

46. Letter from Jamie E. Brown, acting assistant attorney general, to F. James Sensenbrenner, Jr., chair, Judiciary Committee, U.S. Congress, House, May 13, 2003, available online at http://www.epic.org/privacy/terrorism /usapatriot/may03_report.pdf.

47. Quoted in Michael McAuliffe, "Patriot Act Fuels Ire of Book-Lovers," *Springfield Union-News,* January 12, 2003, p. A1, available on Westlaw at 2003 WL 5126485.

48. Quoted in "Patriotic Reading," *Bangor Daily News,* April 9, 2003, p. 8.

49. Quoted in McAuliffe, "Patriot Act Fuels Ire of Book-Lovers."

50. Quoted in Kevin Fagan, "Arcata the Defiant: Town Ordinance Penalizes Officials Who Cooperate with Patriot Act, but Law May Not

Stand Up in Court," *San Francisco Chronicle,* April 13, 2003, p. A17, available online at http://www.sfgate.com.

51. See, e.g., Larry D. Thompson, deputy attorney general, letter to Senate Judiciary Committee, December 2002 (acknowledging that the Patriot Act "changed the standard" from "specific and articulable facts" to "simple relevance"); the relevant passage is cited in "Seeking Truth from Justice," vol. 1, American Civil Liberties Union, New York, July 2003, p. 4, available online at http://www.aclu.org/SafeandFree.

52. See e.g., memorandum to all divisions from the Office of General Counsel, Federal Bureau of Investigation, October 26, 2001, quoted in "Seeking Truth from Justice," vol. 1.

53. The §507 order still requires a certificate of "specific and articulable facts."

54. Statement of Mark Corallo, quoted in William Raspberry, "Homeland Security Sales Pitch," *Washington Post,* July 21, 2003, p. A21. See also J. Patrick Coolican, "Librarians, Booksellers Call for Change to the Patriot Act," *Seattle Times,* February 27, 2004, p. A12 (quoting Corallo as stating, "You have to convince a federal judge," and branding the idea that section 215 allows for fishing expeditions as "false and absurd"); Egelko and Gaura, "Libraries Post Patriot Act Warnings" (quoting Corallo as stating, "One has to convince a judge that the person for whom you're seeking a warrant is a spy or a member of a terrorist organization. The idea that any American citizen can have their records checked by the FBI, that's not true.").

55. "Dispelling the Myths," U.S. Department of Justice, n.d., available online at http://www.lifeandliberty.gov/subs/u_myths.htm.

56. "Statement of Barbara Comstock, Director of Public Affairs, regarding Section 215 OF THE USA PATRIOT ACT," press release, Office of Public Affairs, U.S. Department of Justice, July 30, 2003, available online at http://www.usdoj.gov/opa/pr/2003/July/03_opa_426.htm.

57. Ibid.

58. "The USA Patriot Act: Myth vs. Reality," p. 15 (emphasis added).

59. "Statement of Barbara Comstock."

60. *USA PATRIOT Act,* §§215; 505(a)(2)(B) and (3)(B); 505(b)(2) (2001).

61. See *Brandenberg v. Ohio,* 395 U.S. 444, 447 (1969), holding that the First Amendment does not prevent the punishment of those who advocate the use of force "where such advocacy is directed to inciting or producing imminent lawless action and is likely to incite or produce such action."

62. See *Muslim Community Association of Ann Arbor et al. v. Ashcroft,* Civil No. 03-72913 (E.D. Mich. 2003), affidavit of the Muslim Community Association of Ann Arbor; see also, in the same case, complaint at ¶¶77, 140, 152.

63. Ibid., complaint at ¶113; "Patriot Act Fears Are Stifling Free Speech, ACLU Says in Challenge to Law," press release, American Civil Liberties Union, New York, November 3, 2003, available online at http://www.aclu.org/SafeandFree/SafeandFree.cfm?ID=14307&c=262.

64. "Statement of Barbara Comstock."

65. *Doe v. Ashcroft.*

66. Ibid.

67. See, e.g., *Antiterrorism Tools Enhancement Act of 2003,* HR 3037, 108th Cong., 1st sess., *Congressional Record* 149, no. 123 (September 9, 2003): H 8081, §3 (2003); *Judicially Enforceable Terrorism Subpoenas Act of 2004,* S 2555, 108th Cong., 2nd sess., *Congressional Record* 150, no. 87 (June 22, 2004): S7178–80, §2 (2004).

68. Statement of Rachel Brand, principal deputy assistant attorney general, before the Judiciary Committee, U.S. Congress, Senate, "Tools to Fight Terrorism: Subpoena Authority and Pretrial Detention of Terrorists," 108th Cong., 2nd sess., June 22, 2004, text available online at http://kyl.senate.gov/legis_center/subdocs/062204_brand.pdf.

69. The bills both provide that the proposed administrative subpoena would have to be signed by "the Attorney General," but they leave unclear the extent to which that official would be free to delegate the authority to subordinates, including agents in FBI field offices.

70. Statement of Brand, "Tools to Fight Terrorism."

71. One proposal for modestly enhanced reporting would have required the attorney general to report to Congress the aggregate number of U.S. persons targeted for FISA surveillance orders, including orders for electronic surveillance, physical searches, pen registers, and section 215 document access orders, but no details beyond the "aggregate number" would need be disclosed. See *Domestic Surveillance Oversight Act of 2003,* S 436, 108th Cong., 1st sess., *Congressional Record* 149, no. 30 (February 25, 2003): S 2705, §2.

72. *Foreign Intelligence Surveillance Act,* §1862 (a) and (b). More detailed information must be provided on a confidential basis to the House and Senate Select Committees on Intelligence.

73. *Intelligence Reform and Terrorism Prevention Act of 2004,* Public Law 108-458, *U.S. Statutes at Large* 118 (2004): 3638, §6001(a), amending *U.S. Code* 50, §1801(b)(1), at §6002. In addition, the new obligation under the act to disclose significant Foreign Intelligence Surveillance Court decisions interpreting the statute applies to decisions involving section 215 as well as to all the other provisions of FISA.

74. See supra p. 50.

75. *Doe v. Ashcroft.*

76. See, e.g., Wolfe, "Library Surveillance Exclusion Sought."

77. See, e.g., *Chimel v. California,* 395 U.S. 752, 762 (1969), quoting *Agnello v. United States,* 269 U.S. 20, 33 (1925). ("Belief, however well

founded, that an article sought is concealed in a dwelling house furnishes no justification for a search of that place without a warrant.")

78. See supra p. 66.

79. Justice Department guidelines, for example, require that "all reasonable attempts should be made to obtain information from non-press sources before there is any consideration of subpoenaing the press" and that there be "reason to believe that the information sought [from the journalist] is essential to a successful investigation." *Branzburg v. Hayes,* 408 U.S. 665, 706–7 and n. 41 (1972). Similarly, recognizing a qualified privilege upon the part of a reporter to avoid compelled disclosure when the information sought is not material, critical, and unobtainable from other sources, see *Application of Behar (Church of Scientology v. IRS),* 779 F. Supp. 273 (S.D. N.Y. 1991). Cf. *Matter of Sullivan,* 167 Misc. 2nd 534, 635 N.Y.S. 2nd 437 (Sup. Ct. Queens County 1995); *In re Grand Jury Subpoenas Served on National Broadcasting Co., Inc.,* 178 Misc. 2nd 1052, 683 N.Y.S. 2nd 708 (Sup. Ct. New York County 1998); *In re Ayala,* 162 Misc. 2nd 108, 616 N.Y.S. 2nd 575 (Sup. Ct. Queens County 1994); *Privacy Protection Act,* Public Law 96-440, *U.S. Statutes at Large* 94 (1980): 1879, codified at 42 *U.S. Code,* §2000aa(b).

CHAPTER 5

1. Similarly, if a property owner is not present when the search is conducted, the police must leave a copy of the warrant—again, so that the property owner is aware of the intrusion and any related seizures that have occurred.

2. *Richards v. Wisconsin,* 520 U.S. 385 (1997).

3. *Electronic Communications Privacy Act,* Public Law 99-508, Title II, *U.S. Statutes at Large* 100 (1986): 1864, codified at *U.S. Code* 18, §2705(a)(2).

4. See *Congressional Record* 149, no. 109 (July 22, 2003): H7289–93, H7299–300.

5. *United States v. Freitas,* 800 F. 2nd 1451 (9th Cir. 1986).

6. *Dalia v. United States,* 441 U.S. 238 (1979).

7. See John Kent Walker, "Covert Searches," 39 *Stanford Law Review* 545 (1987). This is apparently a cumulative, not an annual, total, and the report does not make clear how long a time period it covers.

8. E.g., *Dalia v. United States* (upholding installation of electronic bug); compare *United States v. Freitas* (finding insufficient need for clandestine search of suspected methamphetamine laboratory).

9. *United States v. Villegas,* 899 F. 2nd 1324, 1336 (2nd Cir. 1990).

10. *United States v. Freitas,* at 1456.

11. *United States v. Villegas,* at 1337.

12. Ibid.

13. *United States v. Freitas,* at 1456; *United States v. Johns,* 948 F. 2nd 599 (9th Cir. 1991).

14. *United States v. Freitas,* at 1456.

15. *Foreign Intelligence Surveillance Act,* Public Law 95-511, *U.S. Statutes at Large* 92 (1978): 1783, codified at *U.S. Code* 50, §§1823-24. Prior to the Patriot Act, however, such searches were allowed only when they were conducted for "the purpose" of acquiring foreign intelligence information.

16. *Electronic Communications Privacy Act,* §2705(a)(2).

17. See letter from Jamie E. Brown, acting assistant attorney general, to F. James Sensenbrenner, Jr., chair, Judiciary Committee, U.S. Congress, House, May 13, 2003, available online at http://www.epic.org/privacy/terrorism/usapatriot/may03_report.pdf.

18. "The USA Patriot Act: Myth vs. Reality," U.S. Department of Justice, September 2003, p. 12, available online at http://www.nunes.house.gov/PatriotAct.htm.

19. *PATRIOT Oversight Restoration Act of 2003,* S 1695, 108th Cong., 1st sess., *Congressional Record* 149, no. 137 (October 1, 2003): S 12283–85.

20. *Benjamin Franklin True Patriot Act,* HR 3171, 108th Cong., 1st sess., *Congressional Record* 149, no. 123 (September 24, 2003): H 8905.

21. H. Amdt. 292 (A007) to *Departments of Commerce, Justice, and State, the Judiciary, and Related Agencies Appropriations Act,* 2004, HR 2799, 108th Cong., 1st sess., *Congressional Record* 149, no. 109 (adopted July 22, 2003): H 7289.

22. *Protecting the Rights of Individuals Act,* S 1552, 108th Cong., 1st sess., *Congressional Record* 149, no. 116 (July 31, 2003): S 10672, §2. Virtually identical provisions are included in the *Reasonable Notice and Search Act of 2003,* S 1701, 108th Cong., 1st sess., *Congressional Record* 149, no. 138 (October 2, 2003): S 12378; and the *Safety and Freedom Ensured Act,* S 1709, 108th Cong., 1st sess., *Congressional Record* 149, no. 138 (October 2, 2003): S12384–85.

23. This limitation is proposed in all three of the bills cited in note 22, supra.

24. *Uniting and Strengthening America by Providing Appropriate Tools Required to Intercept and Obstruct Terrorism (USA PATRIOT) Act,* Public Law 107-56, *U.S. Statutes at Large* 115 (2001): 272, §213(b)(1).

25. That is the standard set in such cases as *United States v. Freitas,* at 1456, and *United States v. Johns.*

26. See *Protecting the Rights of Individuals Act,* §2; *Reasonable Notice and Search Act of 2003;* and *Safety and Freedom Ensured Act.*

27. See "Issuance of an Order for a Pen Register or a Trap and Trace Device," *U.S. Code* 18, §3123(a).

28. Although the pre–Patriot Act definition of a "pen register" was specifically limited to communications by telephone, the definition of a "trap-and-trace device" was arguably broad enough to encompass Internet communications. See Orin S. Kerr, "Internet Surveillance Law after the USA Patriot Act: The Big Brother that Isn't," 97 *Northwestern University Law Review* 607, 633 (2003).

29. *USA PATRIOT Act,* §216(c)(3).

30. *Smith v. Maryland,* 442 U.S. 735, 744 (1979) (emphasis added). Presumably, the Court meant that numbers recorded by telephone company equipment were accessible to the company's employees. But phone companies ordinarily permit their employees to have such access only for legitimate business purposes. Although the privacy of dialed numbers remains vulnerable to the snooping of rogue employees, that should no more defeat Fourth Amendment protection of privacy than the risk of burglary should defeat legitimate expectations of privacy in one's home.

31. See, e.g., "The USA Patriot Act" (hereafter cited as "EPIC Report"), Electronic Privacy Information Center, Washington, D.C., pp. 5–6 (last updated March 21, 2005), available online at http://www.epic.org/privacy/terrorism/usapatriot.

32. "The USA Patriot Act: Myth vs. Reality," p. 18.

33. See Kerr, "Internet Surveillance Law after the USA Patriot Act," p. 643.

34. *Kyllo v. United States,* 533 U.S. 27 (2001) (thermal imager that reveals heat pattern in private home); *United States v. Karo,* 468 U.S. 705 (1984) (beeper that reveals presence of chemical canister in private home).

35. "The USA Patriot Act: Myth vs. Reality," p. 17.

36. See, e.g., *Terry v. Ohio,* 392 U.S. 1 (1968). Statutory regimes often use the "specific and articulable facts" standard as a threshold requirement as well. See, e.g., *Electronic Communications Privacy Act,* §2703(d) (requirements for court order granting access to stored electronic communications).

37. *Electronic Communications Privacy Act,* §2703(d).

38. See Robert A. Pikowsky, "The Need for Revisions to the Law of Wiretapping and Interception of Email," 10 *Michigan Telecommunications and Technology Law Review* 1, 73–75, 77 (2003).

39. *USA PATRIOT Act,* §216(b), amending *U.S. Code* 18, §3123(a)(3)(A).

40. Because an e-mail message is transmitted through the ISP's server, the reasoning of *Smith v. Maryland* could conceivably be invoked to support the position that e-mail content (having been "voluntarily . . . 'exposed' to [the ISP's] equipment") carries no reasonable expectation of privacy and therefore might not be protected by the Fourth Amendment at all.

41. *Independent Review of the Carnivore System: Final Report,* IIT Research Institute, Lanham, Md., December 8, 2000, pp. 4-3, 4-4, available online at http://www.usdoj.gov/jmd/publications/carniv_final.pdf.

42. FBI internal e-mail, dated April 5, 2000, quoted in Stephen J. Schulhofer, *The Enemy Within: Intelligence Gathering, Law Enforcement, and Civil Liberties in the Wake of September 11* (New York: The Century Foundation Press, 2002), p. 42.

43. *Independent Review of the Carnivore System*, p. xiii.

44. Ibid., pp. xiv–xv.

45. *Omnibus Crime Control and Safe Streets Act*, Public Law 90-351, Title III, *U.S. Statutes at Large* 82 (1986): 197, codified at *U.S. Code* 18 (1968), §2511(2)(a)(1).

46. See, e.g., EPIC Report, supra note 31, p. 8.

47. *Federal Rules of Criminal Procedure*, as amended to December 31, 2000, Rule 6(e)(2).

48. See Sara Sun Beale and James E. Felman, "The Consequences of Enlisting Federal Grand Juries in the War on Terrorism: Assessing the USA Patriot Act's Changes to Grand Jury Secrecy," 25 *Harvard Journal of Law and Public Policy* 699, 699–700 (2002); Jennifer M. Collins, "And the Walls Came Tumbling Down: Sharing Grand Jury Information with the Intelligence Community under the USA PATRIOT Act," 39 *American Criminal Law Review* 1261, 1264–65 (2002).

49. *USA PATRIOT Act*, §203(a), amending *Federal Rules of Criminal Procedure*, Rule 6(e)(3)(D)(2001).

50. *Federal Rules of Criminal Procedure*, Rule 6(e)(3)(D)(ii)(2004).

51. Letter from Daniel J. Bryant, assistant attorney general, to F. James Sensenbrenner, Jr., chair, Judiciary Committee, U.S. Congress, House, July 26, 2002, available online at http://www.house.gov/judiciary/patriotresponses101702.pdf.

52. Statement of Senator Patrick Leahy, chair, Judiciary Committee, U.S. Congress, Senate, 107th Cong., 1st sess., *Congressional Record* 147, no. 144 (October 25, 2001): S110022, available at http://leahy.senate.gov /press/200110/102501.html.

53. Stewart Baker, "Grand Jury Secrecy Rules Help the Terrorists," *Wall Street Journal*, October 5, 2001, p. A14.

54. *The 9/11 Commission Report: Final Report of the National Commission on Terrorist Attacks upon the United States* (New York: W. W. Norton and Company, n.d.), pp. 72–73, available online at http://www .9-11commission.gov/report/911Report.pdf.; Gerald Posner, *Why America Slept* (New York: Random House, 2003), pp. 73–74.

55. *9/11 Commission Report*, pp. 72–73.

56. See Chapter 2.

57. Statement of Patrick Fitzgerald, U.S. attorney for the Northern District of Illinois, before the Judiciary Committee, U.S. Congress, Senate, in hearings on "Protecting Our National Security from Terrorist Attacks: A Review of Criminal Terrorism Investigations and Prosecutions,"

October 21, 2003, text available online at http://judiciary.senate.gov
/testimony.

58. See, e.g., "How the Anti-Terrorism Bill Puts the CIA Back in the
Business of Spying on Americans," American Civil Liberties Union, New
York, October 23, 2001, available online at http://www.aclu.org.

59. Collins, "And the Walls Came Tumbling Down," p. 1268.

60. Ibid.

61. "Report from the Field: The USA PATRIOT Act at Work," U.S.
Department of Justice, July 2004, p. 9, available online at
http://www.epic.org/privacy/terrorism/usapatriot/doj_report.pdf. These safeguards apply only to grand jury information that identifies a U.S. person.

62. Collins, "And the Walls Came Tumbling Down," pp. 1280–83; Beale
and Felman, "Consequences of Enlisting Federal Grand Juries in the War on
Terrorism," p. 719.

63. Beale and Felman, "Consequences of Enlisting Federal Grand Juries
in the War on Terrorism," p. 719.

64. Collins, "And the Walls Came Tumbling Down," pp. 1280–85.

65. Ibid.

66. "USA Patriot Act: Myth vs. Reality," p. 7.

67. Ibid., p. 8.

68. Ibid., p. 10.

69. Ibid., p. 23.

70. See EPIC Report, supra note 31, p. 9.

CHAPTER 6

1. See Stephen J. Schulhofer, "Checks and Balances in Wartime: American,
British and Israeli Experiences," 102 *Michigan Law Review* 1906 (2004).

2. *Intelligence Activities and the Rights of Americans: Final Report of
the Select Committee to Study Governmental Operations with Respect to
Intelligence Activities,* vol. II: *Intelligence Activities and the Rights of
Americans,* S. Rept. 94-755, 94th Cong., 2nd sess., April 26, 1976, pp. 4, 5.

3. Ibid., p. 6.

4. This is a pre–Patriot Act requirement articulated by such cases as
United States v. Freitas, 800 F. 2nd 1451, 1456 (9th Cir. 1986); and *United
States v. Johns,* 948 F. 2nd 599 (9th Cir. 1991).

5. See *Protecting the Rights of Individuals Act,* S 1552, 108th Cong., 1st
sess., *Congressional Record* 149, no. 116 (July 31, 2003): S 10672, §2;
Reasonable Notice and Search Act of 2003, S 1701, 108th Cong., 1st sess.,
Congressional Record 149, no. 138 (October 2, 2003): S 12378; and the
Safety and Freedom Ensured Act, S 1709, 108th Cong., 1st sess.,
Congressional Record 149, no. 138 (October 2, 2003): S12384–85, §3(a)(2).

6. *In re Sealed Case,* 310 F. 3rd 717, 727 (Foreign Intel. Surv. Ct. Rev. 2002). FISA specifies that when such a search targets a U.S. person, it must be supported by probable cause to suspect a foreign intelligence crime. *Foreign Intelligence Surveillance Act,* Public Law 95-511, *U.S. Statutes at Large* 92 (1978): 1783, codified at *U.S. Code* 50, §§1801(b)(2), 1821(1), 1824(a)(3). The Foreign Intelligence Surveillance Court of Review decision, focused on an application for electronic surveillance, does not mention the special problems posed by physical searches, and the opinion therefore leaves open the possible unconstitutionality of the Ashcroft procedures in that context.

7. *Intelligence Reform and Terrorism Prevention Act of 2004,* Public Law 108-458, *U.S. Statutes at Large* 118 (2004): 3638, §6001(a), amending *U.S. Code* 50, §1801(b)(1).

8. Disclosure of that statistic would have been required by the proposed *Domestic Surveillance Oversight Act of 2003,* S 436, 108th Cong., 1st sess., *Congressional Record* 149, no. 30 (February 25, 2003): S 2705, §2, the bill from which the disclosure provisions of the 2004 act were apparently drawn. But the final version, as enacted, deleted the requirement relating to the number of U.S. persons targeted.

9. When sensitive information is involved, the *Classified Information Procedures Act,* Public Law 96-456, *U.S. Statutes at Large* 94 (1980): 2025, codified at *U.S Code* 18 App. 3, provides a workable mechanism for protecting national security interests while affording defense counsel a sufficient means to present a meaningful adversarial challenge.

10. *Foreign Intelligence Surveillance Act,* §1806(f).

11. See Beryl Howell, "FISA: Has the Solution Become a Problem?" in *Protecting What Matters: Technology, Liberty, and Security since 9/11,* ed. Clayton Northouse (forthcoming, 2005).

12. *In re Sealed Case,* at 735–36.

13. *Foreign Intelligence Surveillance Act,* §§1801(b)(1)(A), 1801(e)(2)(B), 1804(a)(4).

14. In the case of U.S. persons, the Foreign Intelligence Surveillance Court of Review has read the statute as limiting FISA surveillance to cases involving the suspected commission of a foreign intelligence crime. See *In re Sealed Case,* at 735–36. But its opinion apparently leaves open the question of whether that limitation applies in the case of surveillance targets who are not U.S. persons.

15. *NAACP v. Alabama,* 357 U.S. 449 (1958).

16. *The 9/11 Commission Report: Final Report of the National Commission on Terrorist Attacks upon the United States* (New York: W. W. Norton and Company, n.d.), p. 395, available online at http://www .9-11commission.gov/report/911Report.pdf. The commission did not elaborate on the structure and powers of the board it had in mind. For discussion of boards that could serve as possible models, see Harold C. Relyea,

"9/11 Commission Recommendations: A Civil Liberties Oversight Board," Congressional Research Service, August 9, 2004, available online at http://www.fas.org/irp/crs/RS21906.pdf.

17. *Intelligence Reform and Terrorism Prevention Act*, §§1011, 8303–5.

18. *Consolidated Appropriations Act of 2005*, Public Law 108-447, *U.S. Statutes at Large* 118 (2004): 2809, §522(a).

19. *Intelligence Reform and Terrorism Prevention Act*, §1061.

20. The officer for civil rights and civil liberties in the Department of Homeland Security, for example, is not given authority to communicate directly with Congress and is not directed to issue reports with respect to any specific matters (such as programs implemented against the officer's advice); instead, the officer is simply instructed to "ensure that . . . Congress receives appropriate reports." *Homeland Security Act of 2002*, Public Law 107-296, *U.S. Statutes at Large* 116 (2002): 2135, as amended, 6 *U.S. Code* §345(a)(5) (2004). The inspectors general of the various agencies do have authority to publish reports directly, but, again, the authority is vague and at best limited. The inspector general of the Department of Homeland Security, for example, is charged with "provid[ing] convenient public access to information regarding (i) the procedure to file complaints . . . ; and (ii) the status of corrective actions taken by the Department. . . ." Inspector General Act of 1978, *U.S. Code 5* App., §8I(f)(2)(H), as amended by the *Intelligence Reform and Terrorism Prevention Act*, §8304.

21. Under the *Intelligence Reform and Terrorism Prevention Act*, §1061(j), "[N]othing in this section shall be construed to require any consultation with the Board."

22. Ibid., §1061(c)(4).

23. Ibid., §1061(d)(4).

24. Cf. *Congressional Record* 150, no. 139 (December 8, 2004): S 11990 (statement of Senator Jon Kyl, calling attention to the problem but arguing that an independent oversight board would in itself create an unacceptably risk-averse environment).

INDEX

ABOUT THE AUTHOR

Stephen J. Schulhofer is the Robert B. McKay Professor of Law at New York University Law School. From 1986 until 2000 he was director of the Center for Studies in Criminal Justice at the University of Chicago, where he was the Julius Kreeger Professor of Law and Criminology, and he served for many years as a consultant to the United States Sentencing Commission. He is the author of *The Enemy Within: Intelligence Gathering, Law Enforcement, and Civil Liberties in the Wake of September 11* (The Century Foundation Press, 2002) as well as many articles on the nexus between liberty and national security. He also writes extensively on other aspects of police practices, criminal law, and criminal procedure.